I0504163

PETER OBI AND NIGERIA POLITICS

PETER OBI AND NIGERIA POLITICS

BY

PASTOR LEONARD ONYEKACHI OKEKE

ISBN: 9798396121577

TABLE OF CONTENTS

CHAPTER ONE

Introduction

This time last year, no one saw Peter Obi coming. Mentally, Nigerians were preparing for yet another general election in a series dominated since the country's return to democracy in 1999 by the incumbent All Progressives Congress (APC) and its rival People's Democratic Party (PDP). An uninspiring two-horse race seemed all but guaranteed, and voters were more or less set to pull the lever for the lesser of two evils in a long-standing arrangement that had failed to deliver the expected "dividends" of economic relief and social stability, but that no one seemed to have either the ingenuity or the resources to challenge effectively.

All that changed in May, 2022, when Peter Obi, the former governor of the southeastern state of Anambra, sensing that a deal had been done that would eventually sideline him in favor of former vice president and perennial PDP candidate Atiku Abubakar, decided to part ways with the PDP. Obi was, contrary to mythology, no maverick outsider. Having been Abubakar's running mate back in an unsuccessful 2019 presidential bid, he could well have stayed within the party and teamed up with him again, but, this time, Obi resolved not to play second fiddle to anyone. Indications have since emerged that his defection to the relatively unknown Labour Party was not a last-minute thing but a move instigated and fully backed by political elders in the Yoruba heartland desperate to prevent either Abubakar or Bola Tinubu, the political bigwig from the Southwest, from becoming president. Obi's initial move may have stemmed from high-stakes political machinations, but, nonetheless, neither he nor his backers could have anticipated what came next.

In the following months, the odds of Obi becoming Nigeria's next president changed, in a dramatic election season, from totally implausible to not unlikely to very possible, tracking the evolving mood of young people who felt at first that Obi stood no chance against the formidable machine of the old guard before becoming totally convinced that he stood as good a chance as any of disrupting the entrenched two-party system. It was the fervency and energy of these young people, the "Obi-dient" as they came to be known, that drove Obi's startling ascendancy, raising the hope that their candidate could overcome a series of formidable structural hurdles.

Africa in Transition

The Obi-dient was an assemblage of disaffected urban youth, students, trade union elements, celebrities and entertainers, and the rump of demonstrators who had caught the attention of the world during the #EndSARS protests against law enforcement brutality in the closing months of 2020. They were young, social media-savvy, and their energy led to an outpouring of political passion long absent from Nigerian presidential politics. Obi, sixty-one, appealed to them because of his youth relative to the other two major candidates (Abubakar and Tinubu are seventy-six and seventy respectively), his austere exterior and seemingly inexhaustible energy, and the resonance of his political messaging—promising to address youth unemployment and corruption, in short to effect some change in a political system that is widely regarded as stagnant.

Ultimately, Obi came up short, coming third behind Abubakar and Tinubu, the president-elect who, in addition to astutely crafting a winning cross-regional coalition, profited from deep division within the PDP. Rejecting the outcome of the presidential election, both Obi and Abubakar have promised to seek legal remedy. This week, Obi made good his promise when he urged the Presidential Election Petition Court in Abuja (FCT) to "either declare him the president-elect or nullify the entire election" and order a fresh one.

Yet, in a fundamental sense, and notwithstanding the outcome of their legal challenge, Peter Obi has already won. In the first place, he has established the viability of a third-party candidacy, something that the sheer entrenchment of the two-party system had made highly unlikely. Second, Obi has effectively ended the political career of 76-year-old Abubakar, a perennial presidential candidate and stalwart of the political process, making him pay a stiff price for initiating the process that led to the fracturing of the opposition PDP. Contrary to the unwritten agreement on power sharing according to which it was the South's turn to produce the president, Abubakar in 2022 blindsided Obi and the rest of the field and secured the nomination for himself. At the moment, curiously, both Abubakar and Obi find themselves in a similar position—both believing themselves cheated out of the presidency. They may well be fighting for the same prize, but it is difficult to believe that they are ultimately engaged in the same struggle. Unlike Abubakar, Obi, sixty-two in July, still has the rest of his political career ahead of him and a real chance of securing the presidency if, among other things, he is willing to do the work to make the Obi-dient a truly pan-Nigerian movement.

For a candidate who at no time presented himself as an ethnic candidate and in fact exercised utmost caution to avoid being defined as one, Obi's success has invigorated hopes of a successful Igbo run for the presidency, a prize that has continued to elude one leg of Nigeria's famed ethnopolitical trident since the conclusion of the Nigerian Civil War in 1970. Part of the reason why many Igbos embraced Obi's candidacy—and why he enjoyed such vociferous support in the heavily Igbo southeastern region—was precisely because the Igbo saw him as an answer to their longstanding yearning to have one of their own in the seat of power. Insofar as the Igbo, perhaps correctly, perceive that exclusion from the presidency was the penalty imposed for the "wrong" of a failed secessionist attempt, Obi was the long-awaited instrument to end their political exile. The ethnic (and to a lesser extent religious Christian) element was a constant undercurrent in the Obi-dient movement, now and again butting against its foundational liberal intent but at no time close to overwhelming it. How this tension is resolved, and which of these dueling tendencies eventually prevails, will go a long way in determining the movement's future.

If Obi can claim moral victory for the aforementioned reasons, his electoral fate seems in retrospect to have been sealed by the very architecture of his candidacy. Breaking away from a political party that he had always been a part of, he alienated himself from the largely Muslim north, widening a regional and political breach that he could not fully repair over the course of the campaign. His abysmal showing in the north will be a painful reminder of what might have been had he been able to cobble together a coalition more palatable to conservative northern power brokers. Having lived by his youth-powered, southern-tending coalition, he had to die by it. Similar to Abubakar, Obi seems to have paid the supreme price for failing to save his political marriage.

Yet another reason for Obi's loss is, paradoxically enough, the Obi-dient. For a movement that, in its best moments, offered a glimpse of what social media allied to liberal-minded political intuitions can be, it was also, regrettably, a study in moral censorship. Holding up Obi as a moral paragon, it refused to entertain any legitimate criticism of the candidate, and in a few instructive cases went as far as attempting to "cancel" those who refused to bend the knee. As it hardened into a political cult more or less, it alienated those who tended to be sympathetic to Obi but had reservations about the rush to beatify him. In not a few cases, genuine attempts to engage were repulsed with peevish name-calling. Trapped in a discursive bubble which made it receptive only to stories of its political conquest and glory, the Obi-dient movement is an object lesson in the dangers of ideological incest. That it can ill afford to continue to harbor this censorious and self-monumentalizing impulse if it aims to broaden its base goes without saying.

What Obi himself does next is also key. If, as most likely, he loses the legal battle, he will be saddled with keeping the movement together for another assault on the presidency in four years, a period within which a lot is bound to change. While he will most likely remain in the affections of young Nigerians, there is no guarantee that the aura currently surrounding him will not fade. Nor should we rule out the possibility of Obi making an unexpected political move, something he has shown a penchant for.

At all events, the election—almost regardless of how the courts eventually rule—is a watershed for Nigeria, a profound challenge to the two-party, region-based power-sharing system, and a moment in which a new youth energy emerges vividly in the electoral sphere. Obi called it an "existential election." What's clearer than the political future of Obi himself is that the Obi-dient movement, having drawn a line in the sand, will henceforth have a say in how the country is governed. In the meantime, it must strive to exorcise its repellent illiberalism.

CHAPTER TWO

Heads of State and Government

An informed discussion of Nigerian federalism against the backdrop of Nigeria's political history characterized by the long years of British Imperialism and thirty years of dictatorial 'native' military rule, and with Emphasis not only on how military rule had emasculated, impoverished And suffocated the proper operation of Nigerian federalism, turning it to An excessively centralized system of governance, but also on what needs to be done to bring Nigeria back to the practice of true federalism. The study believes that "[Reviving the integrity of Nigeria requires a return of maximum federalism... [which recognizes] the authority of the states to have their own Constitutions, police formations...choices of their own capital headquarters...[in addition to the imperative of] redistributing national economic resources in a way that will enable states to develop their natural and human resources".

Forty years after its formal termination, the legacies of colonialism still dominate our lives and public affairs in ways that are insidious and mostly unclear. One main reason for imperialism's prolonged shadows in our lives is that colonialism's most potent stepchild in Nigeria is military rule. Together, British colonial rule and native military rule are responsible for the social formations that have conquered our public affairs and that have created awesome political problems that we seem unable to manage.

One of the most unappreciated aspects of colonialism was its ideological and

intellectual barrier between us and our past traditions. For instance, there was in the

colonial firmament an obstruction between us and our past traditions of governance.

Colonialism magnified its own presence and rendered insignificant the epochs, including

traditions of governance, that were abroad in the West African region before the Arab

and European slave trades devastated our lands, from the sixteenth to the nineteenth

century especially,

DOI: 10.36108/ssan/0002.21.0110

2 Annals of the Social Science Academy of Nigeria, No. 12, January - December, 2000

and before the onset of slave trade's historic successor, namely, European imperialism.

Today, because of the influence of imperial manners of scholarship, Songhai

appears to be historically and spatially distant from us. As a matter of fact, Sqnghai was

our neighbour. Its traditions of politics are important landmarks in any attempt to recapture

a sense of past political traditions in Nigeria. Songhai invaded and ruled several Hausa

states, beginning in 1513, because, in its view, the Hausa states had become unstable and

thus posed a threat to the exercise of peace and justice in the region.

Arab states in the Maghreb of North Africa were troubled by Songhai's strength

and its management of its people's affairs which allowed it to protect the region from

manifest foreign influences. That this is so may be seen from Arab reactions to Songhai's

relations with the Hausa states. Arab immigration into Africa began in 639 C.E., seven

years after the death of Prophet Mohammed. Whereas Arab powers were comfortable

with Songhai's predecessors, Ghana and Mali, Arab influence and interests across the

Sahara had grown considerably by the sixteenth century when Songhai was at the peak of

Its authority. Consequently, Arab states of the Maghreb were ill at ease with Songhai's

Manners of governance (compare Yahya, 1981).

One clear instance of Arab discomfort with Songhai can be seen in the works of

An Arab scholar and traveller of the sixteenth century. Leo African us (whose Arab name

Was Al-Hassan Ibn-Mahanned Al-Wezaz Al-Fasi) was the principal source of information

Available to Europeans on the affairs of West Africa in the seventeenth century. In his

Principal work, he expressed Arab displeasure at Songhai's presence in Hausa lands.

Leo African us had visited Kano and other Hausa territories in the 1520s, enabling him

to comment on Songhai's behaviour as follows: "Afterward", he wrote, "[King Askia of

Songhai] sent governors hither who mightily oppressed and impoverished the [Hausa]

People that were before rich: and most of the inhabitants were carried captive and kept

As slaves by him" (African us, 1600: 828).

Such a characterization of Songhai's relations with its southern neighbours appears

Unduly harsh and probably reflected Arab's intentions on their powerful Black southern

Neighbour. Less than seventy years later, Morocco, the most aggressive of the Arab

States in the Maghreb, invaded Songhai in 1591, sacking its political system and leaving

Behind chaos and mayhem. That was the beginning of the fall of the great traditions of

Politics in our region.

The year 1591 is a crucial demarcation date in our political history. This is so for

two sets of reasons. First, what followed Songhai's fall were smaller states and empires.

Second, such states and empires increasingly became dependent on the goodwill of

Foreign powers. After Songhai, the constant struggle of the states that was already in

Existence in the West African

Region was to stay alive by aligning their practices and principles with Arab, and later,

European powers. Those, like the Hausa states and Benin, that stayed close to their Indigenous traditions of governance lost out. But many states and empires began their Existence in the period after Songhai's fall. These newer emergent political entities Were mostly bereft of the great traditions that informed governance in the West African Region before the collapse of Songhai. Most of these owed their allegiances to alien Arab and European powers and to foreign values of governance.

The significance of these contrasts can best be brought home to all of us by examining the disputes between Hausa Kings and immigrant Fulani leaders that led to the jihad revolt of 1804. They are worth re-examination because the themes of the disputes between the Hausa Kings, who stuck to their native traditions, and the revolutionary Fulani cleric Uthman Dan Fodio appears to have resurfaced in our own times, almost two hundred years after their events. The essential accusation by Uthman Dan Fodio and his younger brother, Abdullah! Muhammad, was that the Hausa Kings were hot faithful to the principles and tradition of governance established in Islam, despite the fact that most of the Hausa had become Moslems for more than four centuries before 1804.

More concretely, the disputes between the immigrant Fulani leaders and the Hausa Kings surrounded two issues that are still relevant to the matter of governance and the problems of federalism in twenty-first century Nigeria. First, Uthman Dan Fodio and Abdullah! Muhammad accused the Hausa Kings of being weak governors who were unable to impose the structures of Islam in their governance. In effect, contrary to the more liberal standards of Hausa Kings, they argued that the state and its government belonged to its rulers. In Fodio's (c.1811: 53) famous words, "The government of a country is the government of its king without question. If the king is a Muslim, his land is Muslim; if he is an Unbeliever, his land is a land of Unbelievers". Or, as he put it in his 1803 jihad memorandum, "the status of a town is the status of its ruler: if he be Muslim, the town belongs to Islam; but if he be heathen, the town is a town of heathendom" (Fodio, c.1803: 240). Fodio quoted with complete approval the warning to the Hausa king of Kano form the Sheikh Abd'Rahman As-Suyuti: "[The King] is the Shade of God ... on the Earth, for verily if he has done righteously, he has the Reward and grateful remembrance, but if he does evil, the Bondage awaits him and his people suffer" (Fodio, c.1811: 57; emphasis added). In Fodio's view, it would be meaningless to consider a state outside its ruler. In effect, the ruler owns the state. According to this view, the king's sins shall be visited upon the inhabitants of his realm. Fodio attacked the Hausa kings and their chiefs in part because they disobeyed this law and failed to recognize its merit.

The second strand of accusation by Uthman Dan Fodio and Abdullah! Muhammad

Was that the Hausa kings were unduly permissive and had allowed, the practice of immoral

Behaviour in their realms. The persistent example of this alleged permissiveness was that women had too much freedom in Hausa society. Hausa Kings sponsored traditional events and festivals in which women were featured prominently. It is important to recognize that women played a major role in Hausa history and society, from ancient times to the nineteenth century. Indeed, the most significant figure in Hausa history is the legendary Queen Amina who came to the throne in about 1588 and ruled the kingdom of Zazzau with many accomplishments, including a record of foreign conquests.

Nonetheless, Fodio was irritated about the high status of women in Hausa society and said as follows: "One of the ways of their government is the evil things which the slavegirls of the sultan [king] and their servants from among the free-born women do in the towns, and they call this jandudu," [which Hiskett explains as] "a dramatization held yearly in which the women and youth of the royal household elected court officials" (Fodio, c.1805: 568). Fodio also accused the Hausa kings of breaching an Islamic law regulating the appearance of women. He said: "One of the ways of their governments is their forbidding to the worshipers of God part which is legal for them, such as the ' veiling of women, which is incumbent upon them" (Fodio, c.1805: 569).

The successful Fulani Revolution ushered into existence the Sokoto Caliphate. It was by far the most important state formation that resulted from the collapse of Songhai. The disputes between its Fulani leaders and the ousted Hausa kings are of very large significance for the political sociology of our region. Despite being Moslem, Hausa kings practiced and plied their indigenous traditions of government that were probably ordained long before the Arabs and Islam arrived in Africa. Such Hausa traditions of government were not far removed from those in existence in indigenous states and empires in Yorubaland, Benin, and other areas of present-day Middle and Southern Nigeria. There are deep-seated principles of government involved in these disputes. They deserve to be restated because they are still unresolved two centuries after the Fulani Revolution in Hausaland in the first decade of the nineteenth century.

The premier indigenous principle of government that was challenged by the Fulani Revolution was about the ownership of the state. Who owns the state? According to the theory-in-use in pre-Revolution Hausaland and indigenous Nigerian states, the state predates royalty and other forms of rulers. The state therefore belongs to the political community. In pre-Revolution Hausaland - as it was in Oyo, Benin, Nupe and scores of other indigenous political systems - the King was a custodian of the state. It was this principle of government that Uthman Dan Fodio directly challenged. In his own words, Nigerian Political History and the Foundations of Nigerian Federalism 5 again, "the government of a country is the government of its king without question".

The second principle of government that was challenged by the Fulani Revolution was that of accountability of rulers. In indigenous states of Nigeria - including the

Hausa states, Benin, Yoruba states, etc., - the ruler was ultimately accountable for his conduct to the people. This principle was particularly enshrined in the Oyo institution of royal suicides by which the Alafin was summoned by the people's representatives to take his own life if he was adjudged to have committed some heinous misdeeds (see Mprton-Williams 1960). Benin history and mythology are riddled with instances of members of the aristocracy who had to commit suicide because of their failures in public affairs (see Okpewho, 1998 and Ekeh, 2000). By contrast, the ruler in Fodio's theory of government was accountable to God through the intervention and interpretation of some theologians, sheiks who are learned in God's ways. Since these theocratic interventions would ultimately lead to Arab authorities, accountability in Fodio's scheme would invoke an allegiance to foreign powers. This was a principle that Songhai disputed with Morocco (Yahy'a, 1981)!

A third major principle at dispute between the Fulani Revolution and indigenous Nigerian principles of government is the status of the individual. To what extent does that state have control over the behavior of the individual? In indigenous Nigeria, groups of kith and kin operate to intervene between the individual and the state. Those who belonged to such king-groups were free men and women. As such, they could hold their own lands and other forms of property. Women's conduct and behaviour could not be dictated by the state. Indeed, in most indigenous Nigerian states and societies, women were powerful interest groups that could strike fear in the hearts of kings. All these fragments of the status of the individual in traditional Hausaland and other regions of indigenous Nigeria were challenged by the Fulani Revolution. First, land was alienated from the Hausa by reason of conquest in the Sokoto Caliphate. Moreover, women lost their freedom to perform public duties, in contrast to their previous powerful status in pre-Revolution Hausaland.

Underlying these alien principles of government is the historic fact that Uthman Dan Fodio's understanding and practice of Islam derive from an early version of the religion that was a lot more conservative than those varieties that were in practice in the Maghreb and in several Arab lands in the nineteenth century. Fodio's version of Islam allows little room for the separation of society from the authority of the state or the separation of State from Church. A primary tenet of Fodio's confession of Islam was its construction of total state and society - as two entities that cannot and ought not be separated, or differentiated, each from the other, in any shape or form.

These are important differences in principles of government. The Fulani Revolution had imported primordial Arab-style principles of government

for whose lack of practice Songhai was in a sense punished by Arabs at the close of the sixteenth century. While these alien principles of government were enforced in conquered Hausaland, officials of the Sokoto Caliphate were more accommodating in other sectors of the Fulani Empire - in northern Yorubaland, Nupe, and even Adamawa. It is important to recognize that these differences predated the arrival of British colonial rule in Nigeria. The Fulani Revolution of 1804 occurred at the beginning of a wild and troubled century in African history. The nineteenth century is forever cursed in our history. It was marked by an unusual amount of violence. It was the century in which the consequences of Songhai's fall finally matured into a horrendous, amount of suffering on the part of the ordinary person in savannah countries of Northern Nigeria. The violence and perfidy of the slave trade had .eaten into the souls of indigenous African states. The principles of government that informed indigenous states in our region were everywhere in danger. Power and violence had replaced authority and legitimacy in many societies of the region. I invite you to read Abubakar Tafawa Balewa's Shaibu Umar. This painful book by the first Prime Minister reveals in a wrenching manner the corruption and violence

that besieged state institutions in the Sokoto Caliphate, as its functionaries engaged in

officially sanctioned slave raids and the slave trade. It offers an avenue for examining

the Arab slave trade across the Sahara and the roles that various government officials

and even clerics played in the management of the trans-Saharan slave trade. It was all in

that cursed century called the nineteenth.

British imperialists arrived in our lands in these distressed times. Although they

had through their role in the slave trade contributed to the growth of the evil and violence

that were abroad in our region in the nineteenth century, they quickly claimed the moral

ground. Initially, there was little possibility of conflict between indigenous principles

of government and the alien principles of government of the Fulani Revolution. This

was so for two reasons. First, Southern Nigeria and Northern Nigeria were separate

British colony of Northern Nigeria, the areas that it pleased British colonial rulers to

call 'pagan' Northern Nigeria were largely separated from what was termed Emirate

Northern Nigeria - which was made up of the old Sokoto Caliphate and Bornu. In Northern

Nigeria, particularly in the Emirates, the principles of government advocated and practiced

by the Fulani Revolution were largely adopted. Thus, lands were assumed to be owned

by the new British rulers who had usurped the authority of Fulani rulers. However, by

mutual agreement between the new conquerors and the old conquerors, a thesis of dual

conquest was devised whereby the old Fulani conquerors ruled directly while the new

British conquerors assumed the role of indirect rulers. This was the beginning of the

famous doctrine of Indirect Rule that was rationalized as a prime policy of British

colonialism in much of Africa in the middle decades of the 20th

century. This device allowed the old Fulani conquerors to preserve a large portion of the alien tradition of government that was practiced in the Sokoto Caliphate.

In Southern Nigeria, indigenous principles of government were largely respected, although Southern Nigeria traditional chieftains were now accountable to the colonial rulers rather than to their own people. British imperial agents leased lands from communities that owned them in binding legal agreements that were often tested in law courts. Government was far less intrusive in colonial Southern Nigeria than in the British colony of Northern Nigeria. On the other hand, the new colonial arrangements encouraged competition^ leading to the rapid growth of the economy of Southern Nigeria. This was in contrast tot he poor performance of the economy in Emirate Northern Nigeria.

It was on economic grounds that British colonial policy makers based their decisions to amalgamate the two colonies of Northern Nigeria and Southern Nigeria. The man chosen to accomplish amalgamation was the conservative British officer Frederick Lugard who conquered Northern Nigeria and devised the theory of dual conquest and its doctrine of Indirect Rule. In effecting amalgamation, Lugard sought to import into Southern Nigeria two key principles of colonial rule in Northern Nigeria. First, he brought with amalgamation the doctrine of Indirect Rule that was crafted in Northern Nigeria. This was largely accepted and was. successful in Southern Nigeria. Second, Lugard fought hard to import into Southern Nigeria the land policy that was inherited from the Fulani Revolution and that was adopted by British colonial rule in Northern Nigeria, namely alienation of land from individuals and their communities/ Unexpectedly, this attempt was fiercely resisted everywhere in the South, leading Lugard to abandon his efforts in this respect.

The land issue was the closest opportunity under colonialism for testing the coexistence of indigenous principles of government in Southern Nigeria and those of the Fulani Revolution and Emirate Northern Nigeria. But any such tests were quashed by a major machinery of British imperialism in Africa. British colonial rulers banned politics. They substituted public administration as the preferred way of conducting the colony's public affairs. Public administration was a hierarchical mode of operating the colonized without gaining their consent. But colonialism in Nigeria was public administration on the cheap in which traditional rulers were sanitized by the colonizers ,and effectively employed as agents of colonial administration. Because politics were banned and criminalized in colonial Nigeria until the 1950s, the traditional rulers who empowered colonial administration had limited political input in policies guiding public administration. This common attribute of colonialism informed the conduct of public affairs in all segments of colonial Nigeria.

The consequence was that Nigerians' political attitudes were frozen and hidden from the knowledge of their fellow Nigerians for more than half a century. Southerners knew very little of the political situation of the Emirate North; nor did the Fulani and other leaders in Emirate Northern Nigeria know much about the Southern neighbours. As Kirk-Green (1968) has well intimated, the first meeting at the Ibadan Conference of 1950 between Southern and Northern leaders was painful because of their ignorance of the political ways of the other Regions. But the 1950 Ibadan Conference was the first thaw in the frozen politics of colonial Nigeria. As it turned out, the entire decade of the 1950s was devoted to decolonization in which Nigeria political leaders for the first time framed the national question and attempted to provide a solution .to its mandate. What was the national question as seen by pioneers of Nigerian politics in the decade of decolonization? Ahmadu Bello, great grandson of Uthman Dan Fodio, Nnamdi Azikiwe, the American-educated Igbo intellectual, and Obafemi Awolowo, the accomplished Yoruba leader, were all knowledgeable men who understood that there were daunting differences in political values and traditions among the various segments of colonial Nigeria. They deserve to bear the title of Founding Fathers of the Nigerian Federation. Above all, they and their followers understood that there were major political differences between Emirate Northern Nigeria and indigenous Southern Nigerian. The national question for them was as follows: Given these profound differences and yet given the exigencies of their common existence and experiences under British colonialism, should Nigerians stay together or should they annul Frederick Lugard's Amalgamation, as Ahmadu Bello once threatened?

The contents of this national .question were complicated by new developments following the expansion of politics as the decade of the 1950s matured. If there were only three solid groups, of Yoruba, Igbo, and Emirate Northern Nigeria in existence, the national question would have been transparent. But British colonial Nigeria was ruled in three regions in which there were ethnic minorities that were culturally sophisticated. Their political oppression by the Igbo in Eastern Nigeria, by the Yoruba in Western Nigeria, and by the Fulani aristocracy in Northern Nigeria complicated the national question in ways that confounded differences in political traditions and principles of government (see Colonial Office, 1958)

Such differences between the South and the North and between majority and minority ethnic groups quickly led to the choice of federalism by 1954 as an avenue of allowing the different regions of Nigeria to rule themselves in their own unique ways (see Arikpo, 1967). The choice of federalism arose from domestic circumstances of differences in the histories of pre-colonial and colonial times. Federalism is rare in Africa. Of the various other attempts to create federal states in British colonial history of Africa – in

Nigerian Political History and the Foundations of Nigerian federalism 9

East, Central, and Southern Africa, none was successful. Nigerian federalism was thus unique. It was at once a testament to the success of Amalgamation of the North and South and to the unwillingness of the Regions of Colonial Nigeria to go their separate ways. But it was also remarkable that differences among these groups were big enough to disallow a unitary form of government.

The form of federalism that emerged in the 1950s was bottom-heavy. In effect, the Regions ceded some amount of authority to the Federal Government, while retaining major economic means and political authority in the Regions. For instance, Nnamdi Azikiwe did not need binding permission from the Federal Government to found the University of Nigeria, Nsukka, ,in the late 1950s. Nor did Obafemi Awolowo and Ahmadu Bello need such permission before founding the University of Ile-Ife(now Obafemi Awolowo University) and Ahmadu Bello University at Zaria respectively. Importantly, each of the three constituent Regions, as well as the Midwest Region when it was created in 1963, had its own Constitution, apart from the common Federal Constitution. Such arrangements allowed the three Regions to employ principles of government that are acceptable to their people. For instance, women voted in Southern elections but were disfranchised in the Northern Nigeria.

But Nigeria federalism was bedeviled right from its beginning by lack of experience in the give and take of politics. Traditions of national politics are acquired from continuous practices and usage. In the political history of colonial Nigeria, such practices were lacking because British colonial rulers banned politics and even criminalized them. The small window of the 1950s for practicing politics was clearly inadequate for establishing a tradition of national politics. Instead, at independence in 1960, the dominant tradition of politics was expressed in notions of conquest of the opponent's powers. Threats and violence replaced discussions and compromises. Respect for the people's vote was scanty in every corner of the country. All of these might well have been remedied and domesticated through repetitive practices of. politics in the post-Independence era if they were accompanied with further discussions and mutual compromises. But the military intervention of 1966 changed the nature of Nigerian public affairs and our practice of federalism. Forcible military rule also changed the character of the national question completely. In a sense, native military rule pushed us backwards to the mode and restrictions of alien colonial rule in a vicious manner. Nigeria's military rule was a stepchild of colonial rule. The military's physical

Formation and modes of operation were consciously modeled on those of the British. But its origins were different from the history of the British military. The Nigerian Military had no tradition of protecting the state and its people from external enemies. Nor was there any well-developed norm of subordination to civil authorities that had Emerged from English history. The

10- Annalsof the Social Science Academy of Nigeria, No. 12, January-December, 2000

Nigerian military was, on the contrary, primarily formed to protect the colonial state From internal native enemies. Like most pristine colonial institutions, it had a latent Loyalty to British manners of action and tended to despise Nigerian traditions of Organization.

When the military seized power in 1966, it immediately took two steps that Showed its colonial credentials. First, it banned and criminalized politics, in ways that Were more direct and more punitive than. British colonial rule ever attempted. Apart From killing leading politicians, it hounded and humiliated others. All elected legislative Assemblies, including those in local councils, were dissolved and banned. Once more, Nigerian public affairs were reduced to administrative fiats. Traditional rulers were once More agents for carrying out the administrative mandate of military rule. These measures

Were continued throughout the course of military rule. Indeed, they became more Thorough going as military rule advanced in Nigeria's political history.

The second immediate action of the military on driving civilians from power in 1966 was to abolish Nigerian federalism, replacing regional powers with a single unitary Government which ruled from one single capital, as it was during vintage colonial times Before the decolonization experiments of the 1950s. As matters turned out, this action Abolishing Nigerian federalism proved to be the Achilles' heel of the new military rulers. The theory and notion of Nigerian federalism had apparently been implanted in Nigerian Minds. Within the military, a counter-coup drove those who urged unitary rule from Power. Thereafter, military rulers, covering more than three decades of post-colonial Nigerian history, respected the label and symbol 'Federal' even while they dismantled The substance of federalism.

A main price which military rulers paid for waging and winning Nigeria's civil War against secessionist Biafra (1967-70) was the promise that they would uphold and Expand Nigerian federalism. While the war lasted, and in the five years following it, Federalism flourished in certain administrative matters, as military chieftains exercised Considerable powers in their regions. But there was heavy resentment within the military Against he permissiveness that this form of administrative federalism entailed. In 1975, Nigeria's wartime military ruler, Yakubu Gowon, who tolerated these diversities (Ekeh, 1992), was overthrown by a military team led by Murtala Muhammed and Olusegun Obasanjo.

CHAPTER THREE

Political Transitions

The thoroughgoing anti-federalist policies and practices of the Nigerian military

Were designed and put in place by the new team, even while retaining the label 'Federal

Military Government of Nigeria'. First, the banning and criminalization of politics became

Ever more entrenched. Second, all vestiges of uniqueness on the part of the constituent

Units of military rule were virtually forbidden. Nigeria Police became ever more

Militarized while any vestiges of local control of the Nigerian Police disappeared. Local

government practices

Nigerian Political History and the Foundations of Nigerian Federalism 11

were made uniform and they became directly dependent on the Central Government for

their funding. All regional universities as of the mid-1970s were taken over by the Federal

Military Government, while elementary and secondary educational systems were

streamlined for all of the country. States were created by military fiat in large numbers,

turning the states into provinces that could not be autonomous in policy matters. Ironically,

this 'dynamic' military rule was designed to return Nigeria to civilian rule while

undermining • the foundations of Nigerian federalism.

More dramatically, the new invigorated military rulers succeeded where Fredrick

Lugard failed. Through the Lands Use Decree of 1978, military rule imposed on the

South and practices that had been in the North but that were resisted and absent from the

South. In many ways, this extension of Northern land usage to the whole of Nigeria was

the highest index of the relationship between native military rule and British colonial

rule. One has been the extension of the other. More directly, Obasanjo finally did Lugard

a favour by ensuring that his policy of land reforms, resisted and rejected in the South, would finally be enthroned by means of a military fiat. That policy also delivered a

major blow to the spirit of Nigerian federalism. If the military could attack this age-old

difference between the South and North, no other area of difference appears safe.

One other zone of military policy and practice of government that has affected

both the spirit and letter of federalism is its sponsorship of violence as a valid principle

of rulership. Despite ruling Nigeria for some thirty years, the Nigerian military has not

invented any theories of legitimation other than its control of the implements and

instruments of violence. Violence has replaced dialogue as a means of discussing public

affairs, under its infamous dictum that dissenters would be 'dealt with immediately'.

Outward obedience has replace inner-directed discipline as the expected way of

responding to government dictation. Nigerian public life is now imbued with this vice

of violence, even as a principle of governance. Remarkably, the centralized Nigerian

Police, the only civil policing unit which military rule has allowed in Nigeria, has no

other method of operation other than violence against civilians, turning this once-proud

agency into a distrusted governmental institution. Sadly, the notion that governance

entailed physical power and violence of rulers over the ruled -rather than authority and

legitimacy binding rulers to the ruled in a system of accountability and legitimacy - is a

legacy of military rule that has become pervasive. It is a political disease that Nigerians

will have to overcome. More than any other system of government, the operation of

federalism requires dialogue and compromises, both of which are in short supply in

political usage under military rule (Ekeh, 1997).

All these developments have led to a recasting of the national question in the

image of the military. By the time the military handed power over to a

civilian regime in 1999, the character of Nigerian federalism and the character of Nigerian public affairs had changed dramatically from what they were when the military came to power in 1966. Nigerian federalism is now top-heavy. Power now resides at the center, almost exclusively. Whereas each of the constituent units of the federation had its own constitution at the end of the negotiations for independence in the 1950s, in addition to a federal Constitution, the central Government of Nigeria now permits only one Constitution, a Constitution that was imposed by military fiat. Policing functions are restricted to Federal responsibilities. Education has virtually been taken over by the Federal Government, with the huge absorption of state universities in 1976-79 causing a diminution of standards at this crucial level of education. The Federal Government is so laden with responsibilities that it is overburdened. At best, Nigeria for a long time remained a dysfunctional federation.

Participation in politics has a way of opening up new vistas of discussion and engagement. The entire hundred years of the twentieth century have been the full extent of Nigeria's existence as a national entity. Out of these hundred years, British colonial rule and native military rule banned politics for a total of some eighty years. Nigerians have had the freedom to practice and engage in politics in the decade of the 1950s; for five years in the first half of the 1960s; for some five years in the Second Republic; and now for some two years in the new millennium. It is remarkable that reactions to the new opportunities of politics have clearly indicated that the principles of government that were disputed between Hausa kings and Fulani immigrant leaders two hundred years ago have not been resolved. Once again, the status of women is at play. Clearly, military fiat has not resolved any disputes. Clearly, a top-heavy military form of federalism is not the appropriate response to these political stirrings. In order to address the national question in its new appearance, we need to reform Nigerian federalism.

We must take seriously the meaning of federalism. In a federal system, the

Federal Constitution is ratified by a specified proportion of the constituent states. In a genuine federal system, each constituent unit has its own Constitution in which it decides how many legislative chambers it desires and in which it decides where its capital should be located. Each unit of a proper federal system should be allowed to select and fly its own flag, in addition to the Nigerian flag. If the Boys Scout of Nigeria, the Nigeria Police Force, and the Nigerian Army have their distinct flags, what prevents states from having their own flags? Federalism requires that each level of government exercise appropriate authority in judicial matters, along with a civilian police formation. It is a disgrace that Nigeria has one police establishment. Does -anybody really believe that the Nigeria Police can handle land cases in local communities, settle marital problems between husbands and wives, arrest petty thieves in

remote villages, patrol the highway, catch armed robbers and still be efficient? Where else in the world is such concentration of policing powers practiced? Is it not wiser to confine the Nigeria Police to Federal responsibilities of law and order, leaving state matters to the states, and local matters of law and order to local police? Let no one ridicule our communities by saying they cannot raise police units. Before British colonial rule, our communities had indigenous police formations. At any rate let those that care and can raise their police be so permitted by Federal and State Constitutions.

Above all else, federalism enjoins a notion of justice in which each constituent unit gives to the whole and receives from the whole in some proportion.. In the decade of decolonization, the Founding Fathers of the Nigerian Federation agreed that each constituent unit of the federation shall . develop its economic resources. The military subverted this formulation because of easy access to wealth from petroleum products. The national question must now embody a notion of justice that does not punish states that produce wealth simply because they are so-called minorities. No political system built on such premises of injustice will survive for long. •

In conclusion, let me phrase the matter national question as follows. First, we must recognize that there are differences in principles of government between indigenous Nigeria and Emirate Northern Nigeria that have historically been contested. Along with this deep-seated historic difference, differences between minority ethnic groups and the three large ethnic groups should be recognized and accommodated in resolving the national question. There is no reason why those who promote Sharia should not be given an opportunity to outline the political basis for its existence in any states of the Federation. But there is no reason why those who seek to protect individuals' and women's rights from Sharia's domain cannot outline the grounds for their fears that Sharia resurrects the disputes between immigrant Fulani leaders and Hausa Kings in the jihad revolt of 1804. Nor is there any valid reason for not permitting those in the Niger Delta who argue that their resources are being unfairly nationalized to propose the economic basis for the type of federalism that will accommodate their advocacy. But we must discuss such differences in civil forums. Hiding them form discussions will not resolve them. And such discussion forums need not be confined to Abuja in one fiesta of Sovereign National Conference. Let discussions be carried out in first instances in villages and communities and states of the Federation in a responsible and directed programme of debating the national question.

Second, the national question must embody a reformulation of Nigerian federalism. Federalism was never a luxury in Nigeria. It was a necessity. Military rule has dangerously turned federalism into a disposable luxury. In doing so, it has attacked the very premises on which the survival of Nigeria rests. It has also changed fundamentally the theories of government that animated political discourse in the 1950s. In these ways, the legacies of military rule threaten the very survival of Nigeria. Reviving the integrity of Nigeria requires a return to maximum federalism, retaining the current states as its constituent units.- Maximum federalism includes the authority of the states to have their own Constitutions, police formations, and choices of their own capital headquarters. It also includes redistributing national economic resources in ways that will enable states to develop their natural and human resources. To those who argue that the present states are too weak for such tasks, I would point out that no state in Nigeria is smaller in population nor in land area nor in human endowments than Gambia. Many of our states are much better endowed than Liberia or Sierra Leone.

Third, and finally, the national question requires that we recognize the pervasive and baneful influences of military rule in our history. We urgently need to demilitarize our national institutions and public affairs. For instance, it is unnecessary and unhelpful to place the National Youth Service Corps under military conduct. More broadly, the centralized methodology of development that military rule has enjoined must be turned around in such a manner as to free communities and states to develop according to their endowments and according to their desires and capabilities. The notion that development can only be achieved and directed from a central point in Abuja is unwise. It is a bad legacy of military rule that reverses the wisdom of the Founding Fathers of the Nigerian Federation.

References

Africanus, Leo. (1896) (c. 1600) The History and Description of Africa and the Notable Things Therein Contained. Trans. John Pory (in 1600). New York: Burt Franklin.

Arikpo, Okoi. (1967) The Development of Modern Nigeria. Middlessex,

England: Penguin Books.

Asad, Talal, ed. (1973) Anthropology and the Colonial Encounter. London: Ithaca.

Balewa, Abubakar Tafawa, Sir. (1967) Shauihu: A Novel by Alhaji Sir Abubakar Tafawa

Balewa. Translated and with an introduction and notes by Mervyn Hiskett. London:

Longmans.

Barth, Heinrich. (1859) Travels and Discoveries in North and central Africa. From

the Journal of an Expedition undertaken under the Auspices of H..M's Government,

in the years 1849-1855. By Henry Bart, with notes and extracts from Mr.

Ricardson's account of the expedition, and a sketch of Denham and Clapperton's

expedition, by the American editor. Philadelphia: J. W. Bradley.

Bello, Ahmadu (1962) My Life. London: Cambridge University Press.

Nigerian Political History and the Foundations of Nigerian Federalism 15

Colonial Office. (1958) Report of the Commission Appointed to Enquire into the

Fears of Minorities and the Means of Allaying Them. London: H .M

Dudley, Billy J. (1982) An Introduction to Nigerian Government and Politics

London: Macmillan Publishers.

Ekeh, Peter P. (1990) 'Social Anthropology and Two Contrasting Uses of Tribalism in

Africa'. Comparative Studies in Society and History, 32:660-700.

Ekeh, Peter P. (1992) 'Yakubu Gowon: A Biography.' in Harvey Glickman, Political

Leaders of Contemporary Africa, South of the Sahara: A Biographical

Dictionary. Westport, Conn.: Greenwood Press.

Ekeh. Peter P. (1 997) The Case for Dialogue on Nigerian Federalism' in Peter P. Ekeh,

(ed) Wilberforce Conference on Nigerian Federalism. Buffalo: Association of

Nigerian Scholars for Dialogue.

Ekeh, Peter P. (2000) 'Contesting the History of Benin Kingdom', Research in African

Literatures. 33(3): 1 47- 1 70.

Fodio, Uthman Dan. (c. 1 805). [I] Kitab al Farq. Translated and edited by M.Hiskett,

Bulletin of the School Oriental and African Studies, 23, 3(1960): 558-79.

Fodio, Uthman Dan . (c. 1811). Tanbihu T Ikhwan. Translated and edited by H.R. Palmer,

Journal of the African Society, 13 (1913-14): 411-14; 14(1914-15): 53-9,

185-92.

Fodio, Uthman Dan. (c. 1 803). [2] The Waathiqat ahl al-Sudan: A Manifesto of the

Fulani Jihad. Translated and edited by A.D.H. Bivar, Journal of African History,

2(1 961): 235-243.

Hiskett, M. (1963) 'Introduction', in Muhammad, Abdullahl. (1963). Tazyin al-Waraqat,

ed., M. Hiskett. Ibadan: Ibadan University Press.

Johnston, H.A.S. (1967). The Fulani Empire of Sokoto. London: Oxford

University Press.

Kirk-Greene. A.H.M. (1968). 'Introduction', in Lugard,, Sir F.D. Lugard and the

Amalgamation of Nigeria: A Documentary Record. Compiled and Introduced

by A.H.M. Kirk-Greene. London: Frank Cass.

Lugard, F.D. (1965) [1922]. The Dual Mandate in British Tropical Africa. Mamden,

Conn.: Archon Books.

Lugard, F.D. (1970) [1913-1918]. Political Memoranda: Revision of

Instructions to Political Officers on Subjects Chiefly Political and

Administrative. London: Frank Cass.

Lugard, F.D. (1968) [1912-1919]. Lugard and the Amalgamation of Nigeria: A

Documentary Record. Compiled and Introduced by A.H.Nfl. Kirk-Greene.

London: Frank Cass.

Morton-Williams, Peter. (1960). 'The Yoruba Ogboni Cult in Oyo.' Africa, 30:362

CHAPTER FOUR

THE EVOLUTION OF THE NIGERIAN STATE

THE EVOLUTION OF THE NIGERIAN STATE: AN OVERVIEW Aiguosatile Otoghile, Ph.D Abstract To appreciate the problems the Nigerian nation has faced since independence, an understanding of the nature and evolution of the Nigerian state becomes imperative. The paper takes a critical look at this and concludes that the Nigerian state was established by the British between 1880 and 1914 through a process that involved oppression, suppression and conquest by force. Two sets of forces may be identified in the origin of the Nigerian state. These are the pre-colonial social formations on the one hand and the colonial social formation on the other. The interaction of these two forces gave the Nigerian state a fragile nature. The Nigerian state did not exist before the coming of the British colonial masters. However, it must be emphasized that there was an interaction amongst the various peoples of present day Nigeria before the coming of the white people (Ekundare, 1973). It follows therefore that an attempt to understand the enormous problems (whether democratic or otherwise) facing Nigeria, like any other post-colonial country, must begin with a serious intellectual concern for its historical, political, social and economic foundations. The problems originated from specific historical events, that is, the history of imposed form of colonial rule and the activities of the pre-colonial capitalist domination which has characterized the exploitation and the underdevelopment of the Nigerian potentials. This paper takes a critical look at the evolution of the democratic state in Nigeria with a specific attention paid to the colonial epoch. It is sub-divided into the following sections: • Colonial administration and economic nationalization in colonial Nigeria • Constitutional developments and the emergence of the Nigerian state • Indirect rule, class formation and the emergence of the Nigerian state • Conclusion Colonial Administration and Economic Nationalization in Colonial Nigeria Colonialism is characterized by economic, political and social control or domination (Nkrumah, 1962). Thus, the annexation of one country by another and the application of a superior technological strength by one nation for the subjugation and economic exploitation of a people or another nation constitute outright colonialism. Nigeria came into being in its present form in 1914 when the two protectorates of Northern and Southern Nigeria were amalgamated by Sir (Later Lord) Fredrick Lugard, the architect of British colonialism in Africa. Until this date, these two protectorates in addition to the colony of Lagos were administered as separate colonies. The amalgamation signaled Britain's complete and effective control of what is now Nigeria. "The present unity of Nigeria as well as disunity" writes Coleman is in part a reflection of the form and character of the colonial governments – the British superstructure and the changes it has undergone since 1990 (Coleman, 1986:46). How did the British create Nigeria and what were the implications of their actions? In this section we shall concentrate on the issue of economic nationalization under colonial rule. The nationalization of the economy can be regarded as the most glaring evidence of colonialism. This began in the year 1900 when the control of trade was taken from the Royal Niger Company. With this, Lugard aggressively pursued the British policy of supplanting locally produced items, especially cloth, by import. While tolls were imposed on native manufacturers, imported European manufacturers were exempted. This was a deliberate attempt to discourage the growth and expansion of local industries (Williams, 1976). Knowledge Review Volume 24 No. 1, April, 2012 2 Another manifestation of economic expansion of the colonial state was the introduction of a uniform currency system throughout British West Africa. This was to facilitate the growth of trade. To this end, a currency board was established based on reserves of gold and securities held in London with coins issued against repayments in sterling. Another major economic policy of the colonial administration was the levying of taxes. This represents an important aspect of the nationalization of the economy. It helped to create wage labour force and also generate increased production of export crops. People had no alternative but to work in order to be able to pay their taxes. Thus, the economic structure of the country was shifted from subsistence peasant agriculture to an export-oriented cash crop economy. In the above cash crop oriented economy, the farmers were not allowed to freely market their products. The colonial administration created statutory marketing boards to cover all export crops that were produced in the country. The marketing boards included the Nigerian Cocoa Marketing Board (1947), the Nigerian Groundnut Marketing Board (1949), the Nigerian Oil Palm Produce Marketing Board (1949) and the Nigerian Cotton Marketing Board (1949). These boards ensured the stabilization of prices of the export crops (Hopkins, 1968). The establishment of these marketing boards engendered severe protest from Nigerian. These agitations led the colonial administration to replace the national marketing boards with regional marketing boards in 1954. Despite this regionalization of marketing boards, the colonial state was still in complete control of the export crops purchased by the regional marketing boards (Tomori, 1978:27) In addition to controlling trade, the colonial administration also enacted the so-called obnoxious ordinances. These ordinances which were part of the 1946 Richard Constitution included the Mineral Ordinance, the Public Land Acquisition Ordinance, the Crown Lands (Amendment) Ordinance and the Appointment and Disposition of Chiefs (Amendment) Ordinance. The aim of this was to ensure that mineral exploitation and land utilization were the bona-fide rights of the colonial state. The colonial administration's policy with respect to the exploitation of Nigeria's mineral resources had two main objectives. The first objective was to eliminate oil indigenous mining activities that had existed before the advent of the Europeans. In addition, the colonial state also wanted to exclude foreign and domestic investors from the exploitation of coal resources. Thus, the colonial administration ensured that Nigerian mining industry would be developed not by Nigerians but by the state with the assistance of foreign capital when it became necessary. On agriculture, the colonial state pursued the policy of preventing the growth of white-settler community in Nigeria and any investment of capital in Nigeria agriculture was absolutely forbidden. In fact, in 1911 and again in 1920, the Governor General of Nigeria emphatically rejected efforts by foreign interest to establish plantations in any part of the country. On land, the colonial state preserved the traditional form of land tenure, thus, inhibiting free movement of people. People who moved out in search of jobs now discovered that they could not own land in their new residence. Thus, contradictions erupted between the preservation of traditional land tenure policy and political control of the economy. This, in part, accounted for inter-ethnic and intra-ethnic tensions and conflicts that have plagued the Nigerian political scene ever since. Another contradiction of the colonial administration was the two separate protective policies regarding land ownership between the North and the South. While in the North state power was more evident in that non-Nigerians and non-Northerners were prohibited from acquiring freehold title, in the South, individual land tenure was allowed to develop extensively without state opposition. Aiguosatile Otoghile, Ph.D 3 On transportation, the colonial state only built roads and railways with forced labour to link the seaports at Lagos and Port Harcourt directly with the agricultural and mining centres in the interior. Furthermore, the colonial state discouraged any form of private enterprise. Thus, at independence in 1960, the entire Nigerian economy had been nationalized. In fact, the state had virtually become the economy and as a result, the various and varied Nigerian ethnic groups were thrown into direct competition that had political ramification. Constitutional Developments and the Emergence of the Nigerian State A look at the colonial history of Nigeria would reveal a deliberate attempt on the part of the colonial masters to create divisive tendencies in the country. Despite Lugard's amalgamation of 1914, the colony and protectorate of Northern and Southern Nigeria continued to be administered separately. Each protectorate had a distinct colonial bureaucracy which fought zealously to retain its autonomy. The officials of the two bureaucracies spoke different official languages. In 1939, however, the country was divided into the Colony of Lagos and three groups of provinces – North, East and West were established, each having a Lieutenant Governor who was responsible to the Governor-General in Lagos (Osuntokun, 1979). Substantial powers and functions were devolved to the headquarters of the three groups of provinces. Thus, by the end of World War II, the degree of administrative devolution had been of such magnitude that it almost boiled down to complete autonomy. The Richard Constitution of 1946 strengthened and formalized the administrative devolution and gave each political unit fairly broad powers. Though the Richard Constitution was expected to last for nine years, subject to limited review after the third and sixth year of operation, it did not last long for a number of reasons. Apart from the criticisms levelled against the constitution, the replacement of Richard with Governor Macpherson spelt doom for the constitution and was subsequently replaced with the McPherson Constitution. The McPherson Constitution had its features, merits and demerits. The constitution assigned legislative authority to the regional houses of assembly, established an executive council for the central government and also created a concurrent list of issues over which the central and regional houses could legislate. Despite the above, the Macpherson Constitution also collapsed. The Macpherson Constitution collapsed not only because of its inherent defects but also because of the political crisis at the time. On the first point, it is important to state that Macpherson Constitution had two major defects. It introduced the principle of collective responsibility without creating room for ministerial responsibility. Ministers could not make and execute policies. Secondly, a situation in which each region was dominated by a political party made the operation of the constitution a most difficult task. On the political crisis, it is important to state that two significant political crises were the Eastern Regional crisis of 1953 and the crisis over the motion for self-government in 1956 (Ojiako, 1981). The Lyttleton Constitution replaced the Macpherson Constitution. This constitution essentially provided for separate governors, separate premiers and cabinet, separate legislatures, separate judiciaries, separate public service commission, civil services, marketing boards and development plans (Ezera, 1964). The period between 1954 and 1960 witnessed the process of decolonization in which the emergent nationalist movements tended to identify with and crystallize around the regions and the major ethnic groups. At the approach of independence in 1960, the apparent united fronts which the major ethnic groups projected through nationalist slogans had been transformed into an unhealthy competition for state power. Indirect Rule, Class Formation and the Emergence of the Nigerian State Colonial capitalism came into contact with the different nationalities that make up present day Nigeria at different times. The incursion of colonialism was piece-meal, starting in 1861 with the annexation of Lagos. These nationalities were at different stages of development hence different class The Evolution of the Nigerian State: An Overview 4 structures. The exposure of these different nationalities to colonial capitalism resulted in the emergence of a new set of classes. These new classes came about as a result of the impact of colonialism's indirect rule, economic forces and education. The manpower problem and the fact that as the Selborne Committee of 1888 pointed out that the overriding concern of the British colonial government was to cut administrative cost, led the committee to recommend ruling though the native institutions as the most effective means of keeping to a minimum the cost that would be involved in trying to govern in any other way. The above led to the introduction of indirect rule in Nigeria, which was basically the subtle tele-guiding of the native administrative structures by the British officials in areas of general policies. The success of this policy was based on the degree of centralization of the native administrative structure and the dominance of the ruling class. Thus, it met with an almost complete success in the North that had a homogenous ruling class and in the West that had developed two powerful classes – the petty-bourgeoisie and the feudal landlords. Finally, in the East, it failed because of lack of any centralized political authority and the absence of any dominant ruling class. It is incontestable that colonial rule was founded in order to serve the capitalist and mother country, but its success and continuation in power, given the above variables of manpower problem and its profit means, was largely dependent on the cooperation of the ruling classes in the different communities (Potholm, 1979). The power of these traditional ruling classes was rooted in noncapitalist form of organization. Consequently, the outcome was a curious paradox, the establishment of a capitalist state based and dependent on pre-capitalist institutions. This had two effects: one was to undermine the pre-colonial social-economic structure. For traditional rulers like chiefs and emirs either adapted to the exigencies of the economic order or yielded a good portion of their authority to more business minded individuals. In the absence of a traditional ruling class in the East, there arose the dominance of the merchant capitalists that Western education created in the peripheral economic activities that colonial capitalism left in the hands of the natives. Thus, the pre-colonial socio-economic structure of the Western and Eastern regions was terribly undermined while the status quo was retained in the North. The second effect of the contradiction of the indirect rule system of colonial administration was that it failed to transform societies so as to enable it to cope with the requirements of the new socio-economic order. This effect was inevitably given the profit means-end of colonialism. Thus, a new class of powerful chiefs was created. Furthermore, British government in order to achieve their aim in the colonies broke down the integrated self-sufficient villages and kingdoms and channeled the productive forces of these communities into production of cash crops. This was effectively done by the introduction of coinage, which had become a new medium of exchange and measuring wealth. In the North, taxes were paid with this new medium of exchange. This coinage that was introduced by the colonial government also affected the land tenure system in Nigeria. For although the land tenure system varied from one area of Nigeria to another, it was essentially communal in character and vested on the family, village or town (Nnoli, 1978). The peasant farmer in receiving an allocation of the right to occupy and use a piece of land from the traditional authorities was free to use the land in the way he deserves, so long it does not alienate the land from the community. But with the coming of colonialism, and its money economy, there was gradually a general shift towards individual ownership and the assignment of market value to land which was formerly free (Nnoli, 1978). This resulted in the displacement of the peasants who cannot afford their own land, creating a class of the Limpon proletariats that migrated to the cities doing unskilled and semi-skilled jobs on day pay. Aiguosatile Otoghile, Ph.D 5 One major outcome of the colonial economic policy was the creation of local merchant capitalist who were only interested in accumulation for its survival (Kay, 1975). These local merchant capitalists later metamorphosed into the comprador bourgeoisie who connived with the industrialized Western countries to exploit their country's economy. The predominant position of this class was later to cause monumental crisis for Nigeria. Another factor that led to the reshaping of the class structure of the different Nigerian nationalities was the impact of Western education. The British did not have a national educational policy; rather, they left the Christian missionaries to introduce Western education in the colonies. It is important to underline the motive for the introduction of Western education in the colonies. The British colonial government knew that the introduction of Western education was a sine qua non for the exploitation of the colony. Without this education, there certainly would not have been clerks and technicians to execute those essential tasks in the government and commerce, particularly those the white people could not carry out themselves. Literate Africans were useful in many ways, although too much literacy was considered dangerous and undesirable. A certain amount of (rudimentary) technical training was essential to provide cheap semi-skilled labour but it should not be allowed to continue beyond a given standard or Africans would soon be competing with whites (Turnbull, 1968:96). A few Africans who initially patronized Western missionary education were drawn mainly from the lower strata of the various Southern communities, mainly slaves. This led to the catapulting of these "scums of society" to the position of economic wealth and political power. So, colonial education produced in the Southern Nigeria a class that constituted part of the ruling class but who by the nature of its composition was antagonistic to the traditional ruling class that formed the other part of the ruling class. The compradors came from the lower strata of traditional societies while the later came from the apex. While this was happening in the South, the North was protected from missionary activities and this had the effect of the non-creation of westernized literates in the North. However, the indirect rule system helped to create a class of comprador bourgeoisie in the north made up of mainly traditional rulers. With the approach of independence, the composition of the ruling class changed somewhat. A new political class emerged. The political class evolved from out of all of the pre-eminent Nigerian colonial groups; wealth was required to finance capital campaigns including the dispensation of patronage; the support and sanctions of the traditional rulers were indispensable to assure popular support; and Western-style education would be needed to manipulate new governing systems and effectively to communicate on an intra and inter-national plane (Graff, 1984). The emergence of these classes had monumental implications for the nascent Nigerian society. The immediate pre-independence politics was characterized by the conflicts of these classes and till date, the issue still remains part of the problem of the Nigerian state. The inevitability of political instability within a class society becomes clearer when one realizes that real political stability exists only in society with total class harmony or a near total class harmony. The genesis of political parties in colonial Nigeria can be traced to the Clifford Constitution of 1922 that introduced the elective principle. The constitution made provision for the election of four members – three elected members representing the municipalities of Lagos and one Calabar (Nnoli, 1978). Political parties were now formed to contest for these newly created positions. The major political parties during this period were the Nigerian National Democratic Party (NNDP), the Nigerian Youth Movement (NYM) and the Peoples' Union (PU). The NNDP was formed on June 24, 1923 by the late Herbert Macaulay and his close associates. The major aims of the party were the provision of higher education in Nigeria and the Africanization of the civil service (Sklar, 1963). The Evolution of the Nigerian State: An Overview 6 The NYM which represented another formidable political party at the time is an offshoot of the Lagos Youth Movements (LYM). Formed in 1933 by a group of young educated, radical Nigerians, including Ikoli, Davies, Vaughan and Akinsanya, the LYM's main objective was to protest against the alleged inferior status of the new Yaba Higher College which it was felt should have been of university standard. The name LYM was however changed to NYM in 1937 to give it a national outlook. The main objective of the NYM was to: Unify the different tribes of Nigeria by adopting encouraging means which would foster better understanding and cooperation between the tribes so that they may come to have a common deal (Epelle, 1960:55) The Peoples' Union was formed in 1908 'as a protest association to the imposition of a general rate to finance a new water scheme. It was led by persons like Obasa, Randle and Alakija. It operated a conservative policy as opposed to the radical aims of the NNDP and its leaders believed in gradualism. Its female counterparts were the Women's Union. Finally, political parties in Nigeria at that period could be said to end with the formation of National Council of Nigeria and Cameroon (NCNC) later National Council of Nigerian Citizens, which participated in Nigerian politics till the fall of the first republic. The NCNC came into existence in 1944. Conclusion This paper has so far been tracing the history of the Nigerian state with a specific reference to its evolution under the colonial masters. It shows clearly that the effects of colonial policies on Nigeria's economic development were indeed devastating given the underlying colonial motive of exploitation. The nationalization of the economy had fundamental implications for the nature of politics that post-colonial Nigeria witnessed. It made the state very attractive as it became the major vehicle for socio-economic mobility. The contest for state power became more intense because of a somewhat contradictory policy of decentralization of the administration. Thus, what emerged out of British colonialism according to Ogbeide (1984) was a state structure which had a monopoly over the commanding heights of the Nigeria economy. But this superstructure was contradictory in design since nationalization of the economy was diametrically opposed to the unbalanced tripartite federal polity bequeathed to Nigeria at independence.

References Adigwe, F. (1974). Essentials of government for West Africa, Ibadan: University Press Ltd. Coleman, J. (1986). Nigeria: Background to nationalism; Katnneholn, Broburg and Wistrom Ekundare, R.O. (1973). An economic history of Nigeria, London: Medthuen and Company Ltd. Ekpelle, S. (1960). The promise of Nigeria, London: Pan Books Ltd. Ezera, L.K. (1964). Constitutional Development in Nigeria, Cambridge: Cambridge University Press. Graff, W.D. (1984). Constitution making and elite formation; paper presented at the Department of Political Science and Public Administration, University of Benin, Benin City, Post Graduate Seminar. Aiguosatile Otoghile, Ph.D 7 Hopkins, A.G. (1968). Economic aspects of political movements in Nigeria and Gold Coast 1918-39 In Journal of African History, 1(7),25-38. Kay, G. (1975). Development and underdevelopment: A Marxist analysis, London: Macmillan Publishers. Nnoli, O. (1978). Ethnic politics in Nigeria, Enugu: Fourth Dimension Publishers. Ogbeide, U.E. (1984). The expansion of the state and ethnic mobilization: The Nigerian experience"; Ph.D. dissertation, Vanderbilt University, Nashville, USA. Ojiako, S.O. (1981). Nigeria: Yesterday, today and...; Lagos: Africana Publishers. Osuntokun, J. (1979). The historical background of Nigerian federalism" In A.B. Akinyemi (ed.) Readings on Federalism, Lagos: NIIA. Potholm, C. (1979). The theory and practice of African politics, Englewood Cliff NJ; Prentice-Hall Inc. Sklar, R. (1963). Nigerian political parties: Power in an emergent African nation, Enugu: Nok Publishers. Tomori, S. (1979). Agriculture forestry and fishing" In F.A. Olaloku (Ed) Structure of the Nigerian economy,

London: Macmillan Publishers. Turnbull, C. (1968). The lonely African, New York: Claredon. Williams, G. (ed) (1976). Nigeria: Economy and Society, London: Rex Collins.

In a January 2023 scandal, one of many in the run up to Nigeria's 2023 elections, current presidential candidate, Atiku Abubakar, was accused of siphoning federal government funds to his party, the People's Democratic Party (PDP), while he was vice president between 1999 and 2007. Perhaps even more interesting, however, is the response he provided in a BBC interview with regards to these allegations, saying that they were nothing new.

Atiku (as he's more commonly known) may have been right in more ways than intended. Political finance in Nigeria has a tradition of murkiness and controversy that precedes even the country's independence.

In 1956, four years before independence, the National Council of Nigeria and the Cameroons (NCNC), a leading party in Nigeria's pre-independence period and the First Republic (1963-1966), was investigated by the British Colonial Government for allegations of financial impropriety on the part of the party's leader, Nnamdi Azikiwe, then premier of Nigeria's Eastern Region. Azikiwe had been accused of using £2 million of Eastern Region funds to purchase shares in the African Continental Bank, a company in which he and his family were major shareholders. The colonial government believed this was done to shore up the company's troubled finances and to help fund the NCNC against the Action Group (AG), the leading party in the Western Region at this time. The commission set up to investigate these charges found Azikiwe guilty of misconduct. These findings, however, had limited impact on his popularity, or the popularity of his party, and subsequent elections in the Eastern Region returned both to power with resounding victories. In 1963, Azikiwe would become the first president of an independent Nigeria.

The experience of Nigeria's First Republic provides similar stories. In 1962, in something of a reversal of roles, AG and its leader, Obafemi Awolowo, a previous premier of the Western Region, were accused of using public funds to enrich the party and some of its prominent members, draining the financial reserves of the Western Region Marketing Board by over £8 million. The Commission of Inquiry established to investigate these events found Awolowo guilty. Unlike Azikiwe, however, his political fortunes would not recover from these accusations, and they would play a role in the Western political crisis that led to Awolowo's imprisonment, and that contributed the fall of the First Republic in the January 1966 coup.

The Second Republic (1979-1983) emerging from the Murtala Muhammad/Olusegun Obasanjo regime was mindful of this type of financial misconduct and the destabilizing effects it could have on democracy, enacting more explicit regulations around political finance than had been present during the

First Republic. This regulation banned all foreign funding of political activity in Nigeria and prohibited all associations other than political parties from 'contribut[ing] to the funds of any political party or to the election expenses of any candidate at an election'. This regulation, however, did not explicitly bar corporate contributions to political funds, and set no monetary limits on financial support from any entity. This oversight allowed a flood of money into politics. At one 1982 Lagos fund-raising ceremony, for example, just ten individuals raised N5 million, a sum equivalent to about $7.5 million at that time. This type of fiscal largesse made politics in the Second Republic an extremely lucrative business for those involved, spawning a new class of patron-contractor who invested funds into candidates of their choosing, and reaped the rewards of lucrative contracts and other state favors once those candidates won office. These practices contributed to rampant corruption, which led to the demise of the Second Republic in the 1983 coup that saw Nigeria's current president, Muhammadu Buhari, become head of state for the first time.

The abortive Third Republic (1992-1993) sought to avoid these issues of party funding through the creation of two state funded parties, the Social Democratic Party (SDP) and National Republican Convention (NRC), intended to limit the use of private money in politics. While this may have limited direct party expenditure, some, including Enugu State University's Dr. R.O. Oji, have claimed that individual candidates spent 'over N1 billion' in the 1993 presidential primaries. It may also be seen as no accident that the victor of the 1993 elections, Moshood Kashimawo Abiola, was also Nigeria's richest man. The consequences of this spending and this outcome, however, were never seen, as this republic never came to be.

UNDER UBANGIDA'S UMBRELLA

Approaches to political finance and party funding in the Fourth Republic (1999-present)–Nigeria's most successful attempt at democracy thus far—have been strongly informed by these past failures. Like in the Second Republic, the 1999 constitution explicitly bars political parties from holding any foreign funds or assets. It further establishes Nigeria's Independent National Electoral Commission (INEC) and, in addition to its duties in conducting elections, charges INEC with the responsibility of monitoring party finance through annual reports of 'the accounts and balance sheet of every political party' to be presented to the National Assembly. The constitution also mandates that political parties provide INEC with yearly statements of their accounts and expenditures, and gives the National Assembly powers to sanction individuals contravening regulations around political finance, up to and including disqualifying these individuals from holding public office.

These constitutional provisions have been further expanded through legislation. The regulatory framework around elections in the Fourth Republic has been guided by the 2001 Electoral Act, and four amendments to this, signed in 2002, 2006, 2010 and 2022, each intended to account for social, political and economic change between elections that may influence their conduct. These amendments have allowed such electoral innovations as electronic voting, early primaries, and measures to improve access for voters with disabilities. The amendments have also increased INEC's independence, decreasing constraints on the commission's funds, allowing it a greater degree of control over its internal operations, and, in 2010, endowing it with some ability to sanction parties and individuals for violations of electoral law.

Each of these amendments, since 2006, has also sought to regulate political finance by setting limits on individual donations to political parties and their candidates, as well as on the maximum expenditure for political campaigns. These limits, however, have soared since they were first introduced. For example, the 2006 amendment limited campaign spending to N500 million for Presidential candidates, N100 million for Governorship campaigns, and N20 million and N10 million for elections to seats in the Senate and House of Representatives, respectively. These limits were doubled in the 2010 amendment, such that campaigns for the Presidency could spend as much as N1 billion, and, in 2022, had increased again, allowing a maximum Presidential campaign spend of N5 billion. Additionally, while maximum individual contributions to political campaigns were capped at N1 million in 2006, this limit had increased to a staggering N50 million by 2022.

Political parties have made claims about their sources of funding that suggest compliance with political finance regulation. PDP, for example, outlines in its constitution that the sources of the party's funds include fees and levies collected from party members, loans, proceeds from investments, money given as donations and gifts, and 'other moneys as may be lawfully received by the party'.

Some attention has been given to the cost of party nomination forms, a source of funding included under the fees and levies referenced in the PDP constitution and which, like campaign spending limits, have seen dramatic increases since they were first introduced. In 2007, PDP charged party members campaigning for the Presidency N10,000 for expression of interest forms and N5 million for nomination forms. In 2015, these costs had increased to N2 million and N20 million respectively. Despite these high costs, and while a variety of figures have been put forth for the cost of PDP's bid for the presidency that year, even the most conservative estimates of that campaign's expenditures would have nomination and interest fees represent under one percent of its total cost.

Despite a clear, well-established and enforceable regulatory framework around political finance in Nigeria, and parties' attempts to make their funding mechanisms seem transparent, political parties in the Fourth Republic have consistently shown contempt for oversight of their funds and expenditures. Nigeria's two leading parties, PDP and All Progressives Congress (APC) have never complied with INEC guidelines around the submission of their financial accounts and expenditures. In 2012, the All Nigeria People's Party (ANPP) was the only major political party found to have its 'financial affairs in order', and in 2019, just four of 91 registered parties—the Action Democratic Party (ADP), Liberation Movement (LM), All Grassroots Alliance (AGA) and the Yes Party (YP)—were compliant with INEC deadlines around financial reporting.

The lack of reliable data around the accounts and expenditures of Nigeria's largest parties limits much insight into sources of party funds and the ways that these resources are used in campaigns and other political activities. Some research, however, has used what information has become publicly available to consider this picture, with distressing findings. Sulaiman Balarabe Kura, for example, a researcher at Sokoto's Usmanu Danfodiyo University, suggests that early as 2003, Olusegun Obasanjo's campaign for reelection to the office of Presidency received at least N2 billion in corporate donations. This was double the limits for financial contributions that would be established three years later, and violated the 1990 Companies and Allied Matters Act, which prohibits corporate entities from making political donations. The 2003 Obasanjo/Atiku campaign would raise a total of at least N5.5 billion, exceeding even the limits set in 2022, and which may have included the federal funds Atiku has been accused of embezzling. Individual donors contributed large portions of this sum, with prominent donors, such as a group identifying itself as 'Friends of Atiku' as well as Alhaji Aliko Dangote, Africa's richest man, contributing over N4 billion to the campaign.

Despite their magnitude, no individual was ever sanctioned for these violations of political finance law, likely because PDP was, in this period, far and away Nigeria's dominant political party, with no institutions or rival political groups yet powerful enough to challenge it. That INEC had not yet been given its current prosecutorial role also meant that the responsibility for enforcing political finance law laid solely with the National Assembly, a body where, in 2003, almost two-thirds of all members belonged to PDP. It is difficult to imagine how these individuals would have allowed their party to suffer sanctions for funding activities that directly contributed to their electoral success.

Other prominent politicians in the early years of the Fourth Republic raised similarly large sums of money for their political campaigns. Former Delta State Governor, James Ibori, for example, received over N2 billion for his 2003 reelection campaign. In the same year Bola Ahmed Tinubu, two-term Governor of Lagos state and one of the leading figures in 2023's Presidential race, raised N1.3 billion. Both figures were an order of magnitude greater than the 2006 limits, three years before those limits were set, and both campaigns received substantial amounts of money from wealthy and influential donors and groups.

This flood of money into politics tilted the playing field in favor of well-connected politicians and their parties, who were able to use their connections to funnel resources towards their political ambitions without any fear of consequence. This gave these entities an almost insurmountably competitive edge against their rivals, enabling them to buy larger crowds at rallies, distribute greater amounts of money and material inducements to potential voters, and, on election day, guarantee victory by buying more votes, stuffing more ballot boxes and paying for more violence to intimidate rival candidates and their voters. The chaos of electoral politics in this early period of the Fourth Republic, where every general election until 2011 was marked by widespread irregularity and abuse, meant that these uses of political finance were particularly effective, and generally accepted as legitimate means of political engagement. This conduct weakened Nigerian democracy, eroding the importance of individual votes, and planting seeds for a culture of voter apathy that persists to this day.

Another outcome of these dynamics was the emergence of a new class of political entrepreneur, the godfather, in a role strongly resembling those of the patron-contractors of the Second Republic. These godfathers used the absent enforcement of political finance rules to fund their chosen candidates to a wide range of political positions, and then, after elections, reaped the rewards of their investments in contracts, waivers and other state favors sent their way. In some parts of Nigeria, godfathers were so widespread and so renowned that they began to be known by other names, perhaps most prominently as Ubangida, meaning 'master' in Hausa, reflecting their mastery over the Nigerian political realm. Some people in this role went as far as to brag about the control that it allowed. Chief Chris Uba, a godfather in Anambra State, for example, declared in a 2003 interview that 'I am the greatest godfather in Nigeria because this is the first time an individual single-handedly put in position every politician in the State'.

As the literature around it describes, godfatherism, like other forms of political corruption, harms democracy by putting in power politicians who may feel more indebted to their godfathers than to their constituents, and so may be more likely to pursue the interests of the former against the latter. It further hollows out the image of political office, strengthening perceptions of government positions as vehicles for personal enrichment instead of as means to address social needs. These consequences may cause voters to lose faith in democracy altogether.

CHAPTER FIVE

Elections and Voting

The large sums of money godfathers bring into politics may also perpetuate their existence, as politicians who initially decline their patronage may, after losing to well-moneyed rivals, seek out godfathers to better compete in future elections, contributing to an arms race for political funds regardless of their sources or the consequences of their use. The conflict between godfathers and governance becomes most apparent when beneficiaries of godfathers' funds attempt to break away from their associated influence. When Chris Ngige, a governor of Anambra state, attempted to assert himself against his godfather, the previously mentioned Chief Uba, the state erupted into violence that featured 24 deaths and the governor's kidnap by armed policemen who forced him to sign a letter of resignation at gunpoint. More recently, attempts by former Lagos governor, Akinwumi Ambode, to break away from Bola Ahmed Tinubu's hold on that state's politics caused Tinubu to endorse another candidate, Babajide Sanwo-Olu, against his reelection bid, Ambode's devastating loss to that candidate in state primaries, and a substantial reduction of his status in Lagos politics.

BOURDILLON AND BULLION VANS

The 2015 general elections were a watershed moment in Nigerian politics, not just for the fact that they were the first to see an incumbent president lose a reelection bid, or that they saw the first transfer of power between political parties in the country's history. These elections were also the first where the party with the highest campaign expenditure did not also go on to win the election. Though INEC's report on party finances for the year have not yet been made public, and while available figures vary, sources such as the Westminster Foundation for Democracy and the Leadership News have claimed that PDP spent anywhere between N4.8 billion and N9.7 billion on former president, Goodluck Jonathan's reelection bid. These sources are more consistent for the expenses of APC, the party whose candidate, Muhammadu Buhari, would go on to win the election, and suggest that APC spent around N2.9 billion, a figure well below even conservative estimates of PDP's spend.

This disruption of the relationship between political finance and electoral outcomes may reflect the deep unpopularity of PDP's candidate, and the promise many saw in Buhari, who many Nigerians believed could offer an answer to Jonathan's ineffective handling of corruption and insurgency. APC also attempted to portray their campaign's financing as removed from the godfatherism that had funded previous successful attempts at the presidency, offering new ways for Nigerians of all classes to contribute to the campaign, such as through dedicated bank accounts, internet-based donation services, text messages to dedicated numbers, and the purchase of party ringtones and scratchcards, setting an ambitious goal of raising N10 billion from these types of contributions. These, and the apparent dethronement of some godfathers in the early years of the Buhari administration, such Bukola Saraki in

Kwara State and Rabiu Musa Kwankwaso in Kano, seemed to suggest that this new governing party was making some progress towards removing the instruments of governance from the hands of the country's privileged few.

This progress, however, may only have been surface-level. Despite their multibillion-naira goals, APC was only able to raise N54 million through direct donations, just around 2 per cent of the total amount raised for the Buhari campaign. Additionally, many of the godfathers who suffered losses of their power during Buhari's administration, including Saraki and Kwankwaso, had themselves joined or supported the APC in its campaign against President Jonathan. Their dethronement, then, instead of an APC play against political corruption, may more likely reflect tensions over power and control within the party, as reflected by the years-long standoff between Saraki and the Buhari administration, and Kwankwaso's now-famous feud with this former godson and political successor, Abdullahi Ganduje. That Ganduje remains a powerful APC member, and, in some respects, has become a budding godfather himself, despite his implication in brazen political corruption, lends to a degree of skepticism around the genuineness of APC's anti-corruption and anti-godfather stance.

Perhaps most damning has been the power enjoyed by influential APC godfathers, the most prominent of whom has been Tinubu. Over his two decades at the forefront of Fourth Republic politics, the Asiwaju of Lagos, as Tinubu is also known, has been implicated in a host of controversies around financial misconduct and state capture. Much of this is featured in 'The Lion of Bourdillon', a 2015 AIT film that accuses Tinubu of, among involvement in other crimes, siphoning Lagos State funds towards his own private accounts, fantastically enriching himself in the process. Just five days after it was first aired, a N150 billion libel suit filed by Tinubu banned the film from Nigerian television.

While Tinubu has emphatically denied any financial wrongdoing during his tenure as governor of Lagos or in the years thereafter, he has also failed to ever provide a consistent account for his well-known and immense wealth. He has, however, been considerably less tight-lipped about the ways this wealth has been used. In 2019, amidst controversy over two bullion vans seen leaving his sprawling Lagos mansion on the eve of that year's elections, Tinubu famously quipped 'I have money to spend…if I like, I give it to the people free of charge'. While some of his allies in APC have since attempted to explain this statement away, and have offered some other dubious reasons for the presence of these vehicles at a private residence, this type of event gives Tinubu the appearance of a man prepared to use any and all available financial resources to pursue his political ambitions.

The 2023 elections, and APC's selection of Tinubu as their party's flagbearer, have seen these concerns return to the fore. This started even before primaries, when Tinubu, perhaps worried that he may not receive the endorsement of his erstwhile ally, President Buhari, boldly claimed to have put the President in office. These same concerns arose during APC primaries, when candidates were accused of issuing bribes to party delegates in exchange for their votes. Despite considerable enthusiasm around other figures vying for APC's nomination, Tinubu emerged from these primaries with over five times as many votes as his closest competitor, current vice president, Yemi Osinbajo. This victory was quickly followed by videos posted on social media purporting to show APC delegates cashing cheques received over the course of the primary.

Concerns over the use of money to influence outcomes in the 2023 elections have also been cited as a reason for the federal government's controversial decision to issue new Naira notes, which some believe might limit the money available to politicians and godfathers to coerce voters. Some also believe that this decision was designed to target Tinubu in particular, a belief that has been expressed by some of the former governor's political allies, including current Kaduna governor, Nasir el-Rufai. Tinubu himself seems to have seized on this belief, with increasingly critical comments about Buhari's administration since the new notes were announced, and recently issuing praise for a Supreme Court ruling extending the deadline for the validity of the old Naira notes.

PAST, PRESENT AND FUTURE KINGS OF NIGERIA

While the true goals of the new Naira policy and the veracity of videos claiming to show political corruption may be questioned, both demonstrate many Nigerians' feelings about Tinubu's most vital political asset: his money, and his willingness to use it. These concerns, however, may not be limited to just one candidate. Atiku also stands next to Tinubu as one of the Fourth Republic's most influential politicians, and has been implicated in considerable financial misconduct beyond the scope of this particular story. Kwankwaso, ANPP's candidate, is a former Kano state godfather himself, and, like his successor, is also not free of allegations of corruption. Peter Obi, perhaps the presidential candidate who has been least connected to financial misconduct, may also not be entirely unconnected from godfatherism. Obi has been alleged to have played the godfather role in Anambra, a state where he was governor, and where news outlets such as the This Day newspaper have claimed he helped install his successor, Willie Obiano. Chief Chris Uba, the previously mentioned Anambra godfather, also recently claimed Peter Obi as a beneficiary of his influence in that state, though some of Obi's supporters, like former ambassador, Bianka Ojukwu, have disagreed with this characterization.

With how pervasive godfatherism has been in Nigeria, it may appear difficult to imagine means to separate the Nigerian electoral process from its corroding influence. Some measures discussed in literature, and that may be gleaned from a consideration of the history of Nigerian political finance, however, may help to bring a degree of structure to this political space.

One such measure may be a reassessment of spending limits set on political candidates and their campaigns. It makes little sense that the National Assembly, in 2006, would enact limits that were ten times lower than PDP's campaign spending three years prior, or that the 2022 limits are just around half of some estimates of PDP's expenditure on Goodluck Jonathan's campaign in 2015. The National Assembly may find value in spending limits that flag campaigns with particularly high expenditures but are permissive enough to reflect real conditions in Nigerian politics. These higher limits may also give parties a fair shot at being able to remain competitive while complying with the letter of the law and may encourage them to be more transparent about their spending. It may also be worth reevaluating that the same limits for State and Local Government campaigns are applied in all states, despite considerable social, economic and demographic differences between these. There may be merit in allowing local authorities more involvement in determining the maximum expenditure for campaigns in these types of elections, to better reflect necessary differences their demands between states.

Additionally, the electoral landscape in Nigeria as whole stands to benefit from ongoing trends that have increased INEC's operational independence and ability to fund itself. These, as well as INEC's capacity to sanction individuals and parties that violate laws around political finance should be expanded as much as is possible, to ensure that the commission remains free of partisan considerations, and to strengthen its ability to enforce the already existing regulatory framework around elections, including those pertaining to money in politics. Other bodies established to regulate the Nigerian political space, such as EFCC, may be similarly strengthened and made more independent, as has been the case in recent years. A stronger EFCC would help prevent large political donors, godfathers and otherwise, from using their contributions to pressure elected officials into prioritizing their interests over those of the Nigerian public, and better protect whistleblowers who bring instances of abuse to the attention of authorities.

Finally, there is a need to continually engage Nigerian media and civil society around issues of political finance to better hold politicians and their parties to account. Nigerian journalists, activists, and ordinary citizens have shown great courage in holding truth to power and confronting political leaders and their allies about their disregard for the laws they are meant to uphold. While much of this has come at the cost of real human lives, as the case in the Lekki Tollgate #ENDSARS protests in 2020, these voices must be supported in their work, as it is work done on every Nigerian's behalf. Godfathers, like Anambra's Chief Uba, have shown their willingness to wield their power and influence against the public in defense of narrow interests, sometimes with fatal consequences. Those that take risks to stand up against this immense pressure deserve the full measure of our support*

CHAPTER SIX.

Civil Society

may be necessary to start this chapter by emphasizing that the Nigerian State as

we know it today with its distinct geo-political identity is a product of British

colonial imperialism of the mid nineteen century. This must not however be

taken literally to mean that the different ethnic groups that were forced to coalesce into what

we have today as Nigeria had no pattern of socio-political arrangement that met their needs,

because however elementary those arrangements had seemed in the eyes of a cursory

observer they exhibited all the characteristics of any other organized political society of the

time (Nwabueze 1982:2). This clarification has become necessary due to the obviously

jaundiced knowledge peddled by some European scholars that black people, prior to colonial

rule, had no history or principles of conduct. For instance, while Professor Hugh TrevorRoper had been
quoted as saying that, "perhaps in the future there will be some African

history to teach. But at present there is none..." (quoted in Crowder, 1968:10), others more

"benign" than him concede that though there may have been some periods of significant

studies in African history, yet such leaps in history are the effort of the Hermits, a branch of

the white race who they hypothesize had visited the African continent in an earlier period.

This wry logic summarized under the Hamitic hypothesis did not believe that the great

kingdoms, empires, civilizations and distinct administrative paraphernalia found in the

continent at the threshold of colonial imperialism were endogenously evolved. To Seligman

and his European disciples who espouse this Hamitic view, pre-colonial Africans were not

capable of any rational thought of their own (Osagie 2002:1 -2).

Consequently, in this section we will attempt to prove that Africans, Nigerian inclusive, had a glorious past just like the Europeans and the Americans, thus confirming the argument by Afrophiles that the underdevelopment which Africa faces today was not only because she was technological inferior to the former as at the onset of colonialism in the nineteenth century (Crowder 1968:4-5), but also because of the debilitating trans-Atlantic slave trade. According to Osagie (2002:2), this inhuman trade which lasted for more than three centuries greatly destabilized the African continent as able bodied men and women w h o were contributing to the well-being of their different nations were carted away to the America s (Epelle, 2010:3).

Though Nigeria prior to colonial rule has been recorded as having about 250 ethnic groups (Nwabueze 1982:9-10; Epelle, 2010:15) each with its distinct cultural identity, yet scholars have argued that beneath this seeming cultural diversity lies some common attributes especially in the area of political administration where two main types have been distinguished, the centralized and the non-centralized political systems (Igwe 2003:20).

Evolution of Nigeria as A Political Unit Epelte Alafuro 174

In the central political system, power, authority and influence were wielded by an identifiable potentate variously addressed by subjects in his ethnic groups as emir, oba, king, emperor etc and governing from a central location in an emirate, kingdom or empire; while in the non-centralized political system, there was no single identifiable person wielding political power and authority, rather segmentary institutions or different groups of persons performed different but connected administrative functions for the benefit of the society. Among the former group arc ethnic groups in the present Northern and Western parts of the country, while the Ibo ethnic group in the Eastern part of the country and Tiv people in the North central axis fall under the non-centralized political system.

We shall study the pre-colonial institutions along the line of the present geo-political zones which Nigeria is divided into, namely, north-west, north-east, north-central, southwest, south-south and south-east.

The North West Zone

In this zone are states like Sokoto, Zamfara, Kebbi, Kano, Kastina, Kaduna and

Jigawa, and the dominant ethnic groups here are the Hausas (Habe) and the Fulanis. The

Hausas were existing in the afore-mentioned areas before their conquest by Usman Dan

Fodio and his Fulani compatriots in a holy war (jihad) prosecuted from 1804.

The Hausas constitute one of the largest linguistic groups in Africa and one account

estimates them to be over twenty million in Nigeria (Ajayi 2002: 28). There is no unanimity

among scholars as to the origin of the Hausas; circumstantial evidence point to the fact that

they may not originally have been a monolithic group but the result of an amalgam of

Baghama and Zaghawa nomads of the Sahara and Nilotic Sudan migrants from the East who

settled in their present abode circa 1000 AD (Ajayi 2002:28).

Between the 11 th and 18th century state formation among the Hausas took firm root

with the emergence of seven original"Hausa Bakwai" States (Biram, Daura, Katsina, Gobir,

Kano, Rano, and Zaria) and later seven other "Hausa banza bakwaf states (Zamfara, Yauri,

Gwari, Nupe, Ilorin, Kebbi, and Kwarafara) (Ajayi, 2002:30; Igwe, 2003:22). Prior to the

emergence of the city-states of today, the Hausas lived in small hamlets and villages known

as "Kauye" where family and kinship ties were the basis of social organization. Each of these

families was headed by a Maigida (head of house), while the village itself was headed by a

Sarki (king). With the introduction of Islam in the 14th and 15th centuries, the politicoadministrative system of the Hausas underwent some fundamental change. Though the

Sarki was still the political and religious leader of people, since "Islam as a religion

recognizes no separation of church and state" (Crowder, 1968:25), yet beginning from the

era of the Islamic ferment he (the sarki) now had to rule with a council of ministers and

territorial officials whose counsel he could not ignore. These officials are: Galadima (heir to the throne); Madaki or Madawaki (commander in chief); IVaziri (chief minister), Magaji

(lord of the treasury); Dagari (head of the king bodyguards); Sarki Yari (head of the prison),

Sarki Yau Doka (head of the police) among others.

For the administration of justice there were the Alkalis, the Qadis (Khadis) and the

Grand Qadis who asjudges at the various levels of the judicial system interpreted the Quran

and pronounced punishment on offenders.

Ewhition of Siberia as A Political Unit Epelle Alafuro 175

With their conqucst by the Fulani jihadists in the early nineteenth century, the Sarkis were

now deposed and a Fulani head appointed as new ruler (emir). Contiguous villages were also

brought together under an emirate system, and for easy domination each emirate was divided

into districts and each district into villages with heads appointed over each of the levels to

assist the emir in local administration and extraction of taxes from the citizens. The emirates

were coordinated from Sokoto where a caliphate was established and headed by a Sultan.

The major duty of the Sultan was to give guidance from time to time to ensure smooth

operation of the system (Abubakar 1980:304) leaving the emirs to be fully in charge of

administration in their domain- though they can only make laws that are in consonance with

Islamic injunctions.

The Fulanis (Fube), on the other hand are the only ethnic group in Africa without a

definite territory of their own (Ajayi 2002:34). They are said to be migrants from Futa Jalon

highland who dispersed themselves into every West African country beginning from Senegal

and extending into the Upper Nile area in the east.

There are basically two types of Fulanis, the cattle Fulani and the Town Fulani. The

former, as their name suggests, are nomads who move regularly with their cattle in search of

good grassland for grazing and water especially during the dry season; while the latter are the

Fulanis who settled in the conquered post-Jihad Hausa towns with some serving as administrators of the territory and hence, more committed in their practice of Islam. Through

marriages and other social forces an integration of the Hausa and the Fulani have emerged in

the North-west zone of Nigeria so much so that it is common place today to talk of an HausaFulani system.

The North-East Zone

In this zone are states like Bauchi, Borno, Gombe, Yobe, Adamawa, and Taraba.

Many kingdoms and empires held sway in these areas before colonial rule but for our

purpose a study of the KanemBornu Empire will suffice.

According to Ajayi (2002:35), the origin of the first settlers in the Kanem-Bornu

Empire is not very clear, however two accounts have emerged. The first is that the Zaghawa

group conquered a group of nomadic settlers in the area and superimposed their hegemony

over them, while the latter account has it that an Arab hero conquered the people between the

9* and 10,h

centuries AD and consequently established the Saifawa dynasty- a dynasty that is

believed to have ruled for over one thousand years (Ajayi, 2002:35-6; Igwe, 2003:24; Osagie

and Ikponmwosa, 2012:17).

The Kanem-Bornu Empire was a centralized one under a supreme ruler called Mai

who ruled through an imperial council of twelve members called Nokcna- the latter of which

advised the Mai on state policy and ensured the full implementation of such policies at the

provincial level. There were four provinces created for the smooth administration of the

empire, namely, the Northern Province (governed by the Yerima), the southern province

(governed by the Kaigama), the western province (governed by the Galadima) and the

eastern province (governed by the Mestrema (Igwe 2003:24-5; and Osagie and

Ikponmwosa, 2012:17).

Evolution of Nigeria ax A Political Unit lipclle Alafuro 176

Apart from these four provincial governors, who incidentally are the most influential in the Nokena, an interesting aspect of the pi e-colonial Kancm-Bornu administration is the role played by women in the political organization of the state. Among these are the king's mother (Magira), the king's elder sister (Magara), and the king's first wife (Gumsu). It is believed that the influence which these women wielded in the political affairs of the kingdom may have stemmed from the fact that they had privileged access to the king's presence. For while the Magira was in charge of the king's feeding the Magara was in charge of the upbringing of the King's children.

The pre-colonial Kanem-Bor\m people were predominantly fanners and pastoralist who grew millet, potatoes and guinea corn and kept goats and cattle. Their strategic location along the trans-Sahara trade route made them to also become a prominent trading state. The Mai derived state revenue from a tax of tenpercent imposed on each individual's total harvest. Mai suzerainty over the empire continued until the 19th century when it was overthrown by the Shehu dynasty that ruled Bornu until the imposition of British rule. Prominent Mais in the history of the empire were Mai Hume Jilimi, Mai Dunama Dibbalemi and Mai IdrisAlooma (Ajayi 2002:37-8, Osagie and Ikponmwosa 2012:17-8).

The North-Central Zone

At present this zone is made up of states like Benue, Kwara, Kogi, Nasarawa, Niger and Plateau. From this zone we will briefly look at the Tiv ethnic group in the present Benue State. The 7/v, according to Osagie (2002:45), "constitute perhaps the largest single ethnic group in the middle Benue basin of Northern Nigeria". Oral tradition holds that the 7/v originated from a progenitor named Tiv who first settled at Swem before moving on with his associates to their present location.

In terms of political organization, the Tiv had a decentralized system of administration in contrast with their neighbours in the North-West and North-East zones. The basic political unit was made up of families (Tsombor) headed by ciders (Mbavcssen).

The secret society (Mbatsav) also played a key role in the administration of the pre-colonial Tiv society, as "in some cases, two members of the secret society were made principal rulers of every kindred" (Igwe, 2003:27). One of these two members is the Tec, a spokeman of the kindred who is believed to have magical powers that could serve spiritual and legislative purposes; while the other is the Shagba Or who handles executive and judicial duties.

The Tiv people are predominantly farmers, little wonder the Benue area is today considered as the food basket of Nigeria. They planted staple food like millet, sorghum, com and root crops like yam and cassava. They also have local artisans who engage in pottery making, weaving and handicraft.

The South West Zone

This zone has six states namely, Lagos, Oyo, Ogun, Ondo, Ekitiy and Osun who arc mainly Yorubas. According to Osagie (2002:8-10), the origin of the Yorubas is still shrouded in mystery and controversy. One version has it that the Yorubas came from the East (Egypt, Yemen or Mecca), while another version believes they descended from heaven. Whichever

Ewlution of Nigeria as A Political Unit Epelle Alafuro 177

version one subscribes to, the fact is that the Yorubas have inhabited the presented area from about 2000-1000 BC till the present era (Osagie 2003:9).

The Oyo Empire is the most prominent of all the kingdoms that existed in the precolonial Yortiba history. Founded around the 15th century AD, the distinctive characteristics of the empire which was made up of the imperial capital (metropolitan Oyo) and the provincial towns was its system of government which had in-built checks and balances so much so that any attempt by the king to assume unconstitutional powers was met with capital punishment (Osagie 2002:11; Osagie and Ikponmwosa 2012:9). At the head of the vast empire, which at its apogee stretched as far as Dahomey and Ga to the west, was the Alafin (lord of many land), assisted by a council of seven members called Oyomesi (headed by

Bashorwi, the Traditional Prime Minister) who were also the leaders of the seven wards into which the metropolitan capital was divided.

In theory, thz Alafin who lives in the metropolitan city was the fountain of power and authority, the principal executioner of the empire's policies, "and a companion of the gods" who kept an elaborate court of officials made up of priests and eunuchs, but in practice, however, he could not be autocratic as he would be promptly checked by the Oyomesi. In reality so limited were the Alafin powers that he could not declare war or peace without the conventional consent of the Oyomesi. Anything to the contrary will lead to the latter asking him to commit suicide. The Oyomesi also acts as kingmakers. When a ruling Alafin dies, the eligible houses nominate potential successors to the Council (Oyomesi) who now selects the most qualified for the exalted post. Normally, the late Oba's son does not succeed him.

Beside the Oyomesi another influential institution in the Old Oyo Empire was the Ogboni cult made up of free and prominent members of the society. This cult approves such decisions of the Oyomesi as the deposition of an Alafin and mediates in times of disagreement between the former and the latter. Other lesser cults were the Oro and the Egungun which helped in the discharge of the orders of the Ogboni.

At the provincial level, there were the Baales (chiefs) who were responsible for general administration at that level and who owe allegiance to ihcAlafin. They maintained law and order in their territories, protected the kingdom's trade routes and paid tributes to the Alafin as occasion demands.

The empire's army headed by the A are Ona Kakanfo (the commanderin-charge), an appointee of thz Alafin, helped protect the efficient administrative system of the empire.

In spite of all these, the early nineteenth century was not a good time for the empire as a lingering civil crises and the rampaging Fulani Jihadist from Ilorin helped put an end to the glorious reign of the Oyo Empire.

The South-South Zone

This zone comprises of six states namely, Rivers, Cross Rivers, Akwa-lbom, Edo, Delta, and Bayelsa. Our interest in this zone will be the old Benin Empire in present Edo State. There are two versions of how the Benin (Bini) empire came into being. The first is that the Binis came from the area around Egypt and journeyed through lle-Ife till they settled at their present location. The second version has it that their progenitor originated from heaven with a snail shell which he turned down on getting to the earth. From this snail shell fell sonic sand to cover the water and form a piece of land for him. Following from this the first set of

Evolution of Nigeria as A Political Unit lipellc Alafuro 178

kings in the kingdom was known as Ogiso (Sky King). The first Ogiso was known as Igbodo, while the last was Owodo whose son and heir apparent, Ekaladercm was banished from the kingdom thereby leading to a period of interregnum in which the elders established a republican administration headed by Evian. I lowever, the attempt by the latter to will the throne to his son led to a serious political crisis in the kingdom prompting the eldersto send a delegation to the Ooni of Ife to help them with an independent ruler. The Ooni obliged them with his youngest son, Oranmiyan who on arrival discovered it would be difficult for a foreigner to govern the people. He left in frustration afterstaying a while, declaring the place "He ibinu" (Yoruba for "place of anger"), from which the current name "Benin" is derived. On his way home Oranmiyan had an affair with a lady, Erinwinda, daughter of the Enogie (ruler) of Egoyr, a place where he had stopped over. This casual relationship produced a child, Eweka, who is credited with the institution of the extant monarchy. All these was said to have happened around the 12,h

century AD (Osagie, 2002:14-17).

The Old Benin Kingdom had two classes of citizens viz; the noble (Adesotu) and the commoners (Ighiotu). The former were further classified into three groups of title holders, the Uzama, Eghaevbo n 'ogbe (palace chiefs), and Eghaevbo n 'Ore (town chiefs). The Uzama are the seven councilors of the kingdom who also double as the highest ranking officials or the most senior chiefs in the kingdom. They serve as heads of the seven quarters or villages immediately outside the Benin walls. Their leader, the Oliha crowns the Oba on his ascension to the throne. The rivalry that existed between the earlier obas and the Uzamas at the restoration of the monarchy led to the establishment of the other two classes of chiefs by Oba Ewuare. There were three groups or associations in the Ogbe (palace) chiefs, the Iwebo, Iweguae, and the Ibiwe corresponding to palace chiefs in charge of the Oba's wardrobe, oba's household and oba's harem respectively. The Ore (town) chiefs are headed by the Iyase (prime minister).

In addition to his traditional role of creating and/or conferring chieftaincy title, the oba also has the right to appoint his sons as chiefs (Enogie) of outlaying villages. This he does to ensure that these villages and towns remain loyal to him. In the absence of an Enogie an Odionwere (the oldest man in the village) takes charge. These leaders ensured maintenance of law and order and extraction of taxes for the oba's administration. Ascension to the throne was through a system of primogeniture as the oba's eldest son normally succeeds him. In spite of all these enormous powers, the oba was not expected to be autocratic as some checks still exist to guide his actions. The British punitive expedition of 1897 in which Oba Ovarenmwen was deposed and deported to Calabar signaled the beginning of the demise of the empire.

The South East Zone

In this zone are states like Abia, Anambra, Jmo, Enugu and Ebonyi. Igbo is the main language spoken by these people and except for a few groups like Onitsha, Oguta and AW, most other Igbo-speaking pre-colonial societies had a segmentary and decentralized political system. Little wonder they had been described as an acephalous or stateless people

(Osagie and Ikponmwosa 2012:14).

The Ibos did not have any centralized political system; therefore the village was the

basic unit of social life with every element of direct democracy.

At the village level the kindred groups held sway while in the village council all male

adults participated in the political process which, as usual, takes place at the village square.

The council also included some influential persons wielding titles like the Ofo title holders

(who are elders of the various kindred groups that make up the village), and the ozo title

holders who earned their elevated status by virtue of their wealth.

The age grades also performed some obligatory services in pre-colonial Ibo villages

as they serve as the executive organ for village council decisions and enforcement agents for

the decrees of the earth goddess. Beyond the elders, the ozo title holders and the age grades,

the diviners also invoked the spirit of ancestors or that of the gods to settle issues and

determine what course of action to take during difficult periods or time of war. This

egalitarian nature of the Ibo people made the imposition of indirect rule a bit problematic for

the British colonialists in the early part of the 20"' century and to get round this problem the

colonizers created men of authority out of the available interpreters and previously

ostracized people who embraced Christian missionaries. This people were given warrants as

government appointees to help the British colonial officials in their surplus extraction

objective. Consequently, these appointees were called "warrant chiefs", and like Osagie and

Ikponmwosa (2012:16) explained, they later metamorphosed into the Eze, Obi and Red Cap

Chiefs of today.

Meaningand Reason for the Introduction of Colonialism

Many reasons have been adduced for why the white man came to this part of the

world in the nineteenth century to colonize it they range from extension of Christianity to a heathenic race as eulogized by European missionaries (Crowder, 1968:10-11) to the

extension of education cum modernization to a backward and uncultured people (Perham,

1957). Suffice it, however, to say that these explanations are not only escapist and

obscurantist, but also apologetic and superficial as they all carefully avoided the

fundamental reasons that brought the whites to Africa and settled for simplistic

interpretations. The fact is that the operations of the capitalist system in 19"' century Europe

brought the white man to Africa (Ake, 1981:13-26; Epelle, 2010:16). At that time the

capitalist economic system in Europe had advanced to a stage where the export of capital to

foreign lands was ineluctable i f the system was to survive (Lenin 1983). For as at then, due to

the low purchasing power of the European worker (a product of the starvation wages paid

him), there was now surplus (unsold) goods, and coupled with the urgent need for cheaper

sources of raw materials the European capitalists were faced with the option of operating

only within their territory and folding up soon or going into the seemingly risky but virgin

lands of Africa with the high hopes of survival it held for them. And as would be expected

they chose the latter option.

From the above it is obvious that the contradictions of the dynamics of nineteenth

century capitalism in Europe helped in transplanting it into Nigeria and other African

countries, and to effectively do this the European traders "must have the tacit support of their

home government through the formal annexation and domestication of foreign territories in

the form of colonialism" (Epelle, 2010:14).

What then is colonialism, one may ask? According to Epelle (2010:12), it is "the

Evolution of Nigeria as A Political Unit Epelle Alafuro 180

forccful occupalion of overseas territories by European powers of the time as a result of the

need to further their imperialist interest". It started surreptitiously in Africa with the

annexation of Congo (Congo Free State) by King Leopold 11 of Belgium in 1876 (Ake

1981:29) and was given additional impetus by the Berlin Conference (November 1884-Febrary 1885) in which European powers of the day under the guidance of Chancellor Bismarck of Germany arbitrarily partitioned African territory amongst themselves with the area now known as Nigeria falling under British rule (Coleman, 1968:62-3).

British Colonial Administration in Nigeria: An Assessment

Historical Background

Albeit, British contact with present day Nigeria dates as far back as 1849 when the British government appointed Mr. John Beecroft as the Consul for the Bights of Benin and Biafrato supervise trading activities in the area, yet the annexation of the island of Lagos by the British authority in August 1861 via the ceding of the area by Oba Dosunmu (Akintoye'sson) could be regarded as the real beginning of the political and constitutional development ol Nigeria. By 1866 the British authority got firm holds over Lagos (ostensibly for the purpose of stopping the illegal trade in slaves) and declared it as its colony with its own Governor, legislative and executive councils (Coleman 1986:41). The councils were advisory in nature for they were established to assist and advice the Governor on state issues though the latter was not bound by their advice.

Apart from Lagos some other areas within the present Western Nigeria were also acquired by the British during this period. The method used for their acquisition involves hoodwinking the paramount ruler of the area into signing a treaty unilaterally drawn up by the British themselves in exchange for protection, but where the local chief is intransigent the "gun-boat diplomacy" was used to coerce him into ceding his domain (Crowder 1968:47-50).

The Berlin conference of 1884-5 conferred on the British the additional impetus of governing the present Niger Delta areas and she. named it the Oil Rivers Protectorate. Consequently, she gave the areas north of the Niger and Benue rivers to the Royal Niger

Company (headed by Sir George Goldie) under a charter that empowered the company not only to trade in the area but to collect taxes from the people on behalf of the British government and to raise a small standing army for the purpose of furthering British interests. In 1893, the British government extended its influence over the Oil Rivers Protectorate and renamed it the Niger Coast Protectorate (Coleman, 1986:41-2) with Major Claude Macdonaldas its first Commissioner (Crowder, 1968:121).

On January 1, 1900 the British government revoked the charter earlier granted the Royal Niger Company to administer the Niger Districts. By that singular act she took over the districts and proclaimed it the Protectorate of Northern Nigeria placing it under the supervision and control of Lord Fredrick Lugard who was named its High Commissioner. And to effectively administer the territory he immediately introduced the system of indirect rule there.

fw*luiion of Niger ui as A Poll ileal Unit EpeUe Alafuro 181

In the same year (1900) the Oil Rivers Protectorate which had been extended in 1893 to include the valley of both the Niger and Benue Rivers was proclaimed the Protectorate of Southern Nigeria with Sir Ralph Moore as its High Commissioner. The colony of Lagos was placcd under the control of Sir Macgregor.

By 1900 therefore, the present geo-political entity known as Nigeria was more or less divided into three separate entities viz: the Lagos colony, the Protectorate of Northern Nigeria, and the Protectorate of Southern Nigeria each with its own machinery of government. This did not last for long for in May 1906, the Colony of Lagos was merged with the Protectorate of Southern Protectorate and Sir Walter Egerton named its first governor (Coleman, 1968:46).

On January 1, 1914 the two separate areas of political administration were brought together as one through the amalgamation of the Northern Protectorate of Nigeria with the

Colony and Protectorate of Southern Nigeria and placed under the control of Fredrick

Lugard (Coleman, 1968:46). From then there existed a single governor for the united Nigeria

and he was known as Governor-General. I Ie administered the entire country assisted by two

Lieutenant Governors for the Northern and Southern Protectorates of Nigeria and an

Administrator for Lagos colony.

Governors of Nigeria between 1914 and 1960

The colonial governors of Nigeria between 1914 and 1960 were:

Sir Fredrick Lugard 1914-1919

Sir Hugh Clifford 1919-1925

Sir Graeme Thompson 1925-1931

Sir Donald Cameron 1931-1935

Sir Bernard Bourdillon 1935-1943

SirArthur Richards 1944-1948

SirJohn Macpherson 1948-1955

SirJames Robertson 1955-1960

Source: Crowder, 1968.

The British government through its Foreign Office delegates powers of

administration to its colonial governors while the British Colonial Office in London served

as the office of the resort. The colonial governors made policy decisions and carried them out

but were guided and advised in all their activities by the Colonial Office in London and in

some cases by the executive and legislative councils in the colony.

The Executive Council

The executive councils which existed in Nigeria between 1900 and 1948 had three

important peculiar attributes: (i) they were only advisory to the Governor on policy matters;

(ii)they were constituted predominantly by European officials (Nigerian were not appointed into the Executive council until 1943);(iii) they were neither representing the entire country in terms of spread of appointment nor were they representing the people of Nigeria in terms ofintercst.

Evolution of Nigeria as A Political Unit Epelle Alafuro 182

Legislative Council

The legislative council of the Nigerian colonies was empowered to make laws for the country subject to the Governor's assent or approval. It thus implies ihat the Governor could veto any law passed by the legislative council. This he can do in two ways: he could refuse its approval, or he could reserve it by not immediately approving it but first referring it to the colonial office in London for final decision. In this regard, the Secretary of State for the Colonics was the only competent authority to approve the annual budget passed by the legislative council in the colony before it could be implemented.

Before the unification of Northern and Southern Nigeria Protectorates in 1914 only the Colony of Lagos had a small legislative council made up of eleven members: the governor, six officials, two European unofficial and two Nigerians. This council was established in 1881 and existed till the threshold of the introduction of the Clifford Constitution in 1922.

Lugard's Pattern of Colonial Administration

Lord Lugard was the first Governor General of the united (amalgamated) Nigeria and on assuming office he introduced the indirect rule system of administration to the whole country. In addition, he established a larger legislative council which he called the Nigerian Council. This council was made up of total membership of thirty six of which:

23 were European officials

7 were European unofficial businessmen and

6 were nominated Nigerian unofficial

The six nominated Nigerians were:

Chief Henshaw of Calabar

Chief Dore Numa of Warri

The Emir of Kano

TheAlafinofOyo

The EmirofSokoto

Hon. C.A. Sapara Williams

It is worthy to note that the Nigerian Council had no real legislative powers; rather the Governor had all the powers centered on him. Worse still, the attendance of the Nigerian unofficial members had nothing to commend it as the Emirs and Chiefs rarely left their palace. The Council met only 7 times between 1914 and 1921, meaning an average of once every year.

In terms of organization of the country for the purpose of political administration three areas of authority could be easily discerned.

1. United Government at the centre: At Lagos there was a government for all parts of the country. It comprised of the office of the Governor-General (Lord Lugard) which was in-charge of all the common services such as railways, mining, post and telegraphs. It could also make laws for all parts of Nigeria.

2. The Northern provinces: The former Protectorate of Northern Nigeria was divided into six provinces with its headquarters at Zungeru. Each of these provinces was under a Resident, and all Residents were under the political supervision of a Lieutenant Governor.

Evolution of Nigeria as A Political Unit Epelle Alafuro 183

3. The Southern provinces: just like Northern Nigeria, the former Colony and Protectorate of Southern Nigeria was divided into nine provinces and placed under

the supervision of a Lieutenant-Governor who had his headquarters in Lagos. He also had a secretariat to assist him in the task of administering all the provinces. It is worthy of mention that both the Northern and Southern provinces had to pass through the Governor-General in Lagos before having access to the Colonial Office in London.

Operations of Indirect Rule Policy

Northern Nigeria

Sir (later Lord) Fredrick Lugard first introduced indirect rule to Northern Nigeria in 1900. Mere the predisposing factors necessary for the successful operation of the policy were already present. For instance, the emirs' authority throughout the emirate was absolute and unquestionable. There was already an existing and well recognized system of taxation and the Alkali courts jurisdiction was unlimited (Coleman, 1986:51). So, when the indirect rule system of governance with its emphasis on the use of traditional rulers who were respected and feared by their people was introduced it contained nothing that was unpleasant or new to the Northerners - British policies were easily disseminated to the grassroots and taxes expressly collected from them. By and large, the indirect rule system was a profound success in the North and that probably explains its extension to Southern Nigeria after the amalgamation of the country in 1914.

Western Nigeria

In the western part of the country some of the predisposing factors for the successful realization of the policy of indirect rule were either absent or where present, then not powerfully established. There was no pre-existing system of taxation in the pre-colonial Yoruba kingdom, what was akin to them was a system of patronage, tributes and homage where once in a while, and not mandatory, the lower chiefs (Baales) and the rank-and-file populace brought gifts to their Oba in return for his blessings. The Oba himself operated more like a constitutional monarch. He was not autocratic and so does not have the power to unilaterally make laws which all and sundry must obey.

Thus when Lugard introduced the system of indirect rule to the West and discovered that the sub-structural elements that accounted for the success of the system in the North were non-existent here he decided to convert the constitutional monarchs into absolute monarchs. He called them "Sole Native Authorities" and gave them powers which were far above the ones granted them by customs and traditions - much to the utter bewilderment and consternation of the people. The people resisted this subtly, but when the obnoxious alien policy of taxation was brought in the people rioted first at Iseyin in 1916 and later at Abeokuta in 1918. In all, over a hundred people died in the anti-taxation riots killed by Lugard's trained black men, but the policy remained.

Hence relative to the North one can conclude that the policy of indirect rule was a partial (quasi) success in the West (Coleman 1986:51).

Evolution of Nigeria as A Political Unit Epelte Alafuro 184

Eastern Nigeria:

In the Eastern part of the country, the people, prior to the introduction of British rule, had no singular executive head with paramount powers, rather governance was through a decentralized system of council of elders, men of titles, age grades and deities. Worse still, these institutions were not autocratic nor did they levy taxes except when occasions which were already established demand.

Faced with this anti-indirect rule situation the British had to devise their own method of making the environment conducive for the operation of the system. First they created chiefs by warrants of appointments- chiefs whose only claim to legitimacy was by the warrant extended them by the British authorities (hence the tag "Warrant Chiefs"); worse still, some of these warrant chiefs, since they were created by the white-men, were rejected by the people and treated like pariahs. They were scarcely obeyed except when the threat of British reprisals was imminent. Some of the "Warrant Chiefs " too made matters worse by either unnecessarily invoking the powers of the colonial authorities especially on their enemies or using their new status to expropriate ex-gratia revenue from the people (Epelle 2010:15).

Matters came to a head in 1929 when a "Warrant Chief' attempted a head count of men, women and children at Oloko village, near Aba. This the people misconceived as an attempt to include the womenfolk in the obnoxious colonial tax register, and in less than no time irate women broke loose in Aba burning the houses of "Warrants Chiefs" and offices and stores of local European traders and British officials. The riot, popularly tagged "Aba Women Riot of 1929" quickly spread like a harmattan haze and colonial offices in the surrounding districts were not spared. Hence, in summary indirect rule policy in the East was a total failure.

Nationalism

Nationalism can be defined as a state of mind which fills a people's heart with emotive sentiments, feelings and love that translates into positive attitudes and actions for their well-being and that of their state. We will proceed from here to take a look at nationalism in Nigeria from inception. In doing this, we will distinguish between early, later and modem nationalism in Nigeria. This distinction reflects the different stages of Nigeria's nationalism from 1861 when the British had its first formal contact with us to 1960.

Early Nationalism

This includes all the subtle reactions and resistance to the initial British penetration and occupation of the area today called Nigeria; it also includes the reactions of the various nationalities to the imposition of colonial rule which tended to subjugate, disarticulate, and destabilize them socially, economically and politically. In order to get a clear focus on this discourse, we will try to periodize early nationalist activities and treat them under two phases:

(i) Phase I (1800-1900)

(ii) Phase II (1900-1920)

Phase I(1800-1900)

£>TJulian of Nigeria as A Political Unit Epelle Alafuro 1 8 5

This phase covcrs all the resistance and opposition efforts put up by our early leaders and peoples against the initial penetration of the hinterland by the colonialist. These were exemplified in militant actions instigated by nationalistic sentiments against foreign control of their land and territories. Some examples of early resistance against colonial contact include:

1. Opposition activities of pre-colonial Nigerian rulers like-

(i) KingJajaofOpobo

(ii) King Kosoko of Lagos

(iii) The Sultan of Sokoto

(iv) Oba Ovoranmen of Benin

2. The secession of Africans from the Anglican Church to form the United Natives of Africa church in 1891

3. TheAkassa raid of 1895.

Phase II (1900-1920)

Following the extensive imposition of colonial rule in Nigeria in 1900, Nigerians continued to struggle against their socio-economic and political subjugation by the colonialists. These struggles were in form of riots, demonstrations and revolts against perceived colonial oppression and certain policies of the colonial government which emasculated the people. A few examples include.

1. The Lagos riots against the:

(a) 1895 proposed house and land tax, but dropped due to protest (Coleman, 1986:178);

(b) Land acquisition act of 1907 in order to provide sites for official residence;

(c) Water rates imposition in 1908 in order to pay loan and maintenance cost;

(d) Land tenure system of 1912 in 1912-13

2. The Egba uprising of 1918

3. The Aba women riots of 1929

4. The various nativistic movements

LaterNationalisni

Sequel to the economic exploitation, racial discrimination and cultural dislocation wrought by colonialism, a trend which was heightened by the neglect of Nigeria's educated elites in the governance of their country, more and more natives became aware of the ills of colonialism and started questioning its justification. The educated elites especially and the Christian converts, having been exposed to western civilization started to engage in nationalist activities which were all geared towards eventual self-government for Nigeria. It is this stage of nationalism that we refer to as later nationalism. Therefore, simply put, later nationalism includes all the constitutional efforts, activities and initiatives undertaken by Nigerians (both educated and non-educated) geared towards liberating the country from the shackles ofcolonialism with a view to attaining political independence.

Evolution of Nigeria as A Political Unit Epelle Alafuro 186

Certain factors gave rise to the growth of nationalism in Nigeria. These can be put into two categories- external and internal.

External Factors that Influenced later Nationalism in Nigeria

1. Early influence of educated Africans in the Diaspora:

(a) Edward Blyden who wrote between 1862 and 1905 on cultural nationalism

(b) John Payne Jackson who advocated political nationalism through his newspaperThzLagos Weekly Record which he edited between 1890-1918.

(c) Marcus Garvey who advocated militant nationalism through his Universal Negro

Improvement Union and Africa Communities League and also the Garveyite

Movement headed by J. Campbell in Lagos.

(d) William Dubois who advocated subtle nationalism through the Pan African

Congresses he convened in Paris (1919), Lisbon (1923) and in New York (1927).

2. Western Education -Education brought an awareness which made the educated

blacks to enlighten the people. It is from this point of Western education as an eye

opener to non-educated natives that we will understand the activities of the National

Congress of British West Africa (NCBWA) and the West African Students Union

(WASU).

3. The Influence of Christian Missionaries the evangelization mission of the

missionaries gave rise to the Africanization of Christianity with proliferation of

African churches e.g. The United Natives of African Church which was formed by

those who broke away from the Anglican Church in 1891. From then other

African churches sprang up and all of them preached spiritual emancipation as a

precursor to political emancipation.

4. Effects of the 2nd World War

(a) Statist economy: the 2nd world war made the colonialists to control the Nigerian

economy in order to maximize profits; for instance they introduced the Marketing

Boards and started controlling international trade, but this did not go down well with

Nigerian traders hence theyjoined the nationalist struggle.

(b) War time shortages of essential commodities due to lesser imports ultimately led to

local shortages. Since Nigerians were already used to these foreign products, there was now the need to produce them locally especially as the market was readily available. This led to small scale industrialization which was later discouraged after the war thereby further exposing the ills of colonialism since Nigerians now had new insights into what they could do when independent from Britain. This encouraged the business class to engage in nationalist struggles too.

(c) Racial intermingling which'was facilitated by the war made soldiers to move across Africa and mix with the natives of Europe and Asia. This helped the Nigerian soldiers who fought in the war alongside British soldiers to realize that the white man was not a special human being, after all; thus encouraging the former to ask for independence.

(d) Atlantic Charter of 1941 in which the Allied forces engaged in the Second World War agreed to grant the right of self determination to all countries.

Ewlution of Nigeria as A Political Unit Epelle Alafuro 1 8 7

(e) The granting of independence by Britain to its colonies in East Asia after the Second World War.

Internal factors that Influenced Later Nationalism in Nigeria

1. Economic exploitation of the natives by the colonialists

2. Racial discrimination and dehumanization of natives

3. Divide and rule tactics of the colonial government

4. Neglect of the educated elites in the governance of Nigeria.

Instruments of Later Nationalism

Most of the activities of later nationalism were carried out through the instrumentality of certain machinery. These include:

1. Rallies

2. Constitutional conferences

3. Newspapers like the Jackson's Lagos Weekly Record, and Nnamdi Azikwe's West African Pilot.

4. Political parties like Herbert Macaulay's Nigeria National Democratic Party formed m 1923, the National Youth Movement formed in 1934, National Council of Nigeria and Cameroon formed in 1944, etc.

Constitutional Development in Nigeria, 1922-1979

Clifford Constitution of 1922

Sir Hugh Clifford became the colonial governor of Nigeria in 1920 and on assuming office he set about establishing a constitutional framework for his administration. Highlights ofthat constitution were:

• Creation of a legislative council made up of 46 members, 27 of whom including the governor were officials, 9 unofficial European members and 6 Africans both nominated by the Governor-General) and 4 elected Nigerians (3 from Lagos and I from Calabar).

• Introduction of the elective principle that saw to the formation of the first political party in Nigeria, the Nigerian National Democratic Party (NNDP) by Engineer .H. Macaulay, Nnamdi Azikiwe, Ernest Ikoli, Samuel Adesanya etc in 1923. Thus the elective principle saw to the election of the first four Nigerians, and indeed Africans, into government at any level in the history of colonialism in Africa. It also marked the beginning of involving educated elites in governance.

• Creation of an Executive Council made up of the governor and 11 senior official members. It had no African representative, official or unofficial.

The elective principle made for a limited franchise as only British subjects and British protected Nigerians with a minimum income of 100 pounds per annum were eligible to vote and be voted for.

Evolution of Nigeria as A Political Unit Epellc Alafuro 188

Richard Constitution (1946)

Arthur Richard was the colonial governor of Nigeria from 1944 to 1947; but before

him others who had governed the country were Sir Graeme Thompson (who succeeded

Clifford), Sir Donald Cameron, and Sir Bernard Bourdillon, all in that order.

• Although the nationalists were not consulted before the promulgation of the

constitution, it (the constitution) had 3 cardinal objectives:

(i) To promote the unity of Nigeria

(ii) To provide for the diverse interests in the disparate Nigerian protectorates

(iii) To ensure greater participation ofNigerians in their governance.

• To achieve these objectives, the constitution:

1. Provided for the division of Nigeria into a 3 regional structure (North, East and

West) formally because the division started in 1939. This took care of

providing for the diversity of the Nigerian nation state.

2. Creation of Regional assemblies in all the 3 regions; but the North had a bicameral

legislative i.e. I louse of Chiefs in addition to a House of Assembly

3. Retained but enlarged the central legislative council in Lagos to cover the entire

country instead of only the South e.g. membership of the council was 16

official members including the governor and 24 unoffcial members. 4 of this 24

were elected still from Lagos and Calabar and the remaining 20 indirectly elected or

nominated by the regional assemblies (electoral collegiate system).

4. Retained the Executive council but appointed 2 Nigerians to it.

5. Made the centre (federal government) stronger as the regional assemblies played

only advisory roles (the beginning of the lop-sided structure of Nigerian federalism

which skews power in favour of the centre).

6. Retained but reduced the limited franchise provision from 100 pounds to 50 pounds.

7. The unique element of the Richards constitution was the policy of regionalism

Which been retained in subsequent constitutions till date.

Macpherson Constitution of 1951

Sir John Macpherson was the colonial governor of Nigeria from 1948-1954. He saw

the major defect of his predecessor's (Richard) constitution which was lack of consultation

With the people, so he initiated series of consultsation.

Specifically, in line with the above thinking, the constitution had the following

Characteristics:

• Replaced the existing central legislative council with an enlarged body called the

House of Representatives. This House was made up of 136 members half (68) of

which were from the North with the East and West sharing the remaining 68, 34

apiece. The Governor was the President of this body alongside 6 other official

members appointed by the Governor.

• The House of Reps, had powers to make laws for the entire country and such laws

remained substantive in the case of conflict with those made by the regional

assemblies.

E\x\'uti<\n of Nigeria as A Political Unit Epelle Alafuro 1 8 9

• 1 he House also appropriated money (budget) for the entire country and on behalf

ofthe regions.

• It strengthened the 3 regional structure of the Richard s Constitutio n a n d

established in each the office of a Governor.

Retained but enlarged the regional assemblies with an elected, instead of a

nominated, Nigerian majority.

The regional assemblies in the North and West had a bicameral legislative, House of

Chiefs and House of Assembly. They were to make laws subject to the ratification of the House of Reps, at the centre.

• Election to the regional assemblies was through an electoral college whose Membership was elected in a primary election at the local level wherein all male adult Tax-papers were qualified to vote.

• There was provision for a Council of Ministers to replace the Executive council at the centre. The Council of ministers was made up of the Governor who served as its President, 6 official members made up of the 3 Lt Governors, the secretary to the Nigerian government, the Attorney general and the Financial Secretary to the Nigerian Government. The other members were 12 Nigerians, 4 from each of the Regions. The council was collectively responsible for policy making and Implementation.

• The constitution also created Regional Executive councils.

• The regional assemblies were to serve as electoral colleges from which members were elected into the House of reps and the council of ministers in Lagos.

• Established a Public Service Commission for Nigeria which was to advise the Governor on issues of appointment, discipline or dismissal of public officers.

Lyttleton Constitution of 1954

This constitution is also referred to as the Federal Constitution of 1954 because for the first time in Nigeria's constitutional history, it provided for the practice of true federalism. Thus, Nigeria became a federation consisting of three regions, each with its own exclusive powers but with certain powers retained by the centre which governed them all. Of particular note is the fact that the Southern Cameroun's under British trusteeship now became a quasi-federal territory. In addition, Lagos became a federal territory governed directly by the federal government.

The constitution, which came into effect on October 1st 1954 had the following

essential provisions:

The Legislature at Centre

The central legislature (The I louse Reps) was now composed of a speaker, three (3) exofficio members and 184 representative members who were directly elected instead

nomination through the regions as was the case in previous constitutions. The 184 members

were directly elected to represent the regions at the Centre in the proportion of 92 from the

north, 42 each from the east and west, 6 from the Southern Camcroons and 2 from Lagos.

Involution of Nigeria as A Political Unit lip elie Alafuro 190

The Regions

• The Governors no longer presided over the regional legislatures. The Eastern and

Western Mouse of Assembly now had Speakers to do this. Only the North still had an

ex-officio president and 3 other ex-officio members.

• The regions had more autonomy as they were empowered by the constitution to

make laws without recourse to the House of Reps for approval and ratification.

• The regions no longer served as electoral colleges to the House of Reps because

elections were now to be held directly into the House of Reps.

The Executive

• The constitution retained the nomenclature- Council of Ministers, who formed the

executive council. They were appointed from the House of Reps whose

members were directly elected. The constitution also provided for the appointment

of the executive by the Governor-General but on the advice of the majority party in

the region (in most cases, the Premier).

• The constitution provided for the appointment of a Premier for each region. The

Premier was to head the regional executive council.

• Regional ministers were appointed on the advice of the regional Premier.

• The appellations of Governor and Lieutenant Governor were changed to Governor-general and Governors for the center and the regions respectively.

The Judiciary

• There was a Nigerianization and regionalization of the Judiciary such that the

Judiciary was decentralized with the regions having their separate courts.

• The constitution established a Federal Supreme Court which became the court of

highest jurisdiction in Nigeria. This court was composed of the Chief Justice of the

federation and federal justices.

Granting of Self Rule and Parliamentary Democracy

1960 Independence Constitution

On October 1st 1960 the British colonialists granted political independence to the

Nigerian people thereby heralding the beginning of self rule by Nigerian nationalists and

elites. A constitution (Independence Constitution) was promulgated to guide this process.

Features of that constitution are as below.

Essentially, the independence constitution was similar in many respects to the 1954

constitution. The differences stem from important amendments and agreed changes made on

the 1954 constitution during the period 1954-1960. Basically, the independence constitution

drew its inputs from the 1957 and 1958 conferences held in London and Lagos.

The constitution was contained in a big document arranged into 5 schedules. The

first schedule was "Order in council revoked by this Order", the second was "The

Constitution of the Federation of Nigeria" and the third, fourth and fifth schedules contained

the constitutions of the Northern, Western and Eastern N igeria respectively.

Ewlution of MigchaasA Political Unit Epelle Alafuro 191

The following arc specific changes contained in the 1960 Independence constitution.

• Creation of the office of Prime Minister (PM) of the federation. The PM was to be

appointed by the Governor General. The Governor-General was to appoint the person who appeared to him to command a majority in the House of Rep. members.

Part of the duties of the PM was to recommend to the Governor-General, the

Appointment of any membe r of the House of Reps as a minister.

Inter-Governmental Relations

In the power relations between the centre and the three regions, the exclusive lists of

the federal government's functions were expanded to cover 4 items. For example, it

Now included mines and minerals, weights and measures, shipping etc. The

Concurrent list was also expanded to cover a set of 28 items/subjects.

• The constitution also conferred special and emergency powers on the Federal

Government. Emergency here, as defined by the constitution meant.

(a) When the federation is at war

(b) When there is in force resolution passed by each House of Parliament that a state of

Emergency exists.

(c) When each House by a two-third declares "that democratic constitution in Nigeria

are threatened by subversion" (section 65, sub(s) 3a b & c).

• The constitution also provided for an element of incidental power. This aims at

giving to the federal legislative (House of Reps) in regards to its exclusive

powers, and to the regional Houses of Assembly and House of Reps in regard to

their concurrent powers

• However, section 64(4) of the constitution states that when a regional law conflicts

with a federal law, the regional law will, to the extent of its inconsistency,

become null and void.

The Regions

• All powers not in the exclusive and concurrent lists were the sole responsibility of

the region to enable them make for good governance, peace and order in the regions.

- The governor was empowered to remove the Premier if he loses the confidence of the House of Assembly.
- The Premiers at regional level including the Prime Minister at the centre in Lagos were conferred with executive powers.

Thejudiciary

- Provision was made for the appointment of the Supreme Court Chief Justice and high court judges on the advice of the Judicial Service Commission, subject to the approval of the Privy Council.

Evolution of Nigeria as A Political Unit IZpellc Alafuro 1 9 2

- The Federal Supreme Court could declarc regional and federal laws or parts of such laws unconstitutional.

The legislature

- Bicameral legislatures were adopted for the Centre and the East, which before now had a unicameral legislature. The membership of the Lower House at the Centre was now 312.
- The upper house, hereafter called the Senate was composed of 12 members from each of the three Regions, 4 from Lagos as federal territory and 4 special members to be appointed by the Prime Minister.
- The power over money and other bills was given to the Senate and as a result, it could delay money bills and such other financial bills for one month and six months respectively to provide time for quality legislation on such important matters.
- The constitution provided for a parliamentary democratic system of government with the Governor-General being the ceremonial Head of State and a representative of the British monarch, the Queen of England.

Other provisions

• The constitution provided a special procedure for its amendment which thus made

it a rigid constitution. E.g. it provided that the initiative for any amendment

process does not lie with only the centre. The process was, in fact, very elaborate

and cumbersome.

• Provided for fundamental human rights of all citizens, i.e. freedom of movement,

expression, right to life etc.

• Created ana defined Nigerian citizenship

• Made security and police federal concerns.

• Provided for a new revenue allocation formula basedon need, national interest and

even development.

1963 Republican Constitution

This constitution which made Nigeria a republic, i.e. a state ruled by an elected leader and

not a monarch, was enacted into law on 19th September, 1963. Essentially, it retained a good

portion of the 1960 constitution. We will thus concentrate on the new provision of the

constitution emanating from the all parties constitutional conference held in July 1963 in

Lagos.

• The constitution replaced the "Order in Council" provision of the 1960 constitution

with "We the people". This is in line with the goal of erasing all traces

and vestiges of colonialism from our national life.

• Provided for a President who is the Head of State and Commander-in-Chief of the

Armed Forces.

• The President was to be elected through an electoral college of the National Assembly

for a 5 year tenure after which he would be eligible to seek re-election only once.

• The President could appoint ambassadors and perform such other ceremonial

Ewlution of Nigeria as A Political Unit Epelle Alafuro

functions as the Governor-General as the Monarch did in the previous constitution.

The constitution empowered the President to appoint officers of the judiciary on the

advice of the Prime Minister. There wer e constitutional safeguards for the removal of

judicial officers.

The constitution empowered the Supreme Court to be the apex court of Nigeria in

place of the Privy Council in London. The Judicial review content of the Judiciary as

provided by the constitution empowered it, for example, to review, declare null and

void and decide in all matters that had to do with the law.

The constitution also made for the financial independence of the judiciary through the

establishment of the Consolidated Revenue Fund from which benefits and

emoluments of the Judiciary were guaranteed.

There was provision for a Director of Public Prosecution who was answerable to the

Federal Attorney General on the Executive. This was a clear departure from previous

parliamentary conventions and it made for checks and balance.

It outlined the procedures for the creation of more regions (states or units) and

boundary adjustments. One of such procedures was that the motion for such creation

must go through all the parliaments in the land and passed by a two-third majority of

members of same.

Nigeria's 1979 Presidential Constitution: Background and Principles

It is pertinent to note that the making of the 1979 Constitution was informed more by

the sad experiences of the past than hopes of the future. Underlying the Constitution making

process was a deep felt desire to avoid the disasters and disappointments of the First

Republic which led to a military interregnum that lasted from January 1966-October 1979.

Among the factors widely believed to have contributed to the demise of the First Republic were:

(a) the structural anomaly in Nigeria's federal system in which one region was predominant over others thus violating J.S Mills' law of federal stability according to which there "should not be any one state (in a federation) so much powerful than the rest as to be capable of vying in strength with many of them combined".

(b) The debilitating centrifugal pressures exerted by the intense regionalism and tribalism which informed the politics of the First Republic.

(c) The contradictions which developed from the situation in which the need for parties and politicians to achieve powe r at centre was frustrated by the impossibility of transcending their local ethnic group or regional base of political support.

(d) The disaffection created amon g a significant section of the political elite by the failure to grant relative political autonomy to the nation's minority groups.

(e) Finally, the perhaps most importantly, forces and pressures unleashed by intra-elite competition for scarce resources (patronage, appointments, amenities) needed not only for primitive accumulation, but also to satisfy demand emanating from the elites ethnic or regional constituencies.

Evolution of Nigeria as A Political Unit Epellc Alafuro 194

Military in Nigerian Politics

As with most concepts in the social sciences, the term "military" has not been given a one-for-all definition. This problem is not helped by most writers who because of the ubiquitous nature of the military in African politics begin their subject by describing what the military does rather than defining who they are. However, Ake is one of the few exceptionsto this rule. According to him:

The military is... (an) organization for defense of the last resort: defense through violence. It is afighting machine. The military comes into its own when our common humanity and sociability has disappeared in irreconcilable conflict. It comes into its own when two parties confront each other as executioners- to kill or be killed. Because of what it exists to do and the circumstances in which it does it the military formation is essentially constituted in the following way: it is a chain of command whose members are integrated in a strict relationship of subordination and ordination (Ake 1989:26-7).

From the above definition we can deduce the fact that the military is primarily an institution that functions for the sole purpose of defending the territorial integrity of a country. Seen in this perspective it is therefore very clear that they are trained to kill and not to rule. Worse still, their disposition is such that they function in an atmosphere of apprehension, morbid fear and quixotic danger of real and unreal enemies.

One bureaucratic characteristic of the military which Ake's definition has helped in highlighting is their hierarchical structure. Being an institution that is trained to always be on guard for the enemy it is expected that its members must be wielded into a command and control structure that will help enhance alertness, discipline and ensure strict compliance with orders. Hence in the military, officials occupy positions that are stratified in the form of a ladder with each successive position being responsible for those beneath it, while those below are responsible to those above them. Following from this, policy directives which come in the form of orders are issues from above, while the only duty of subordinates is slavish obedience to such orders. Complaints (if necessary) are only entertained after the order had been complied with. Initiative is not only discouraged but seriously frowned at and can carry dire consequences for the "offender".

What all these point to is that the military is not an institution that thrives on consultation and compromise; and since politics on the other hand revolves around consultation and compromise, the only conclusion open to us here is that military

involvement in politics of any country is an aberration. "When the military comes to power it

regards the polity as a chain of command; governance is a matter of commanding and the

chief virtue of citizens, obedience"(Ake 1989:7).

In summary, the military as can be gleaned from the above expose is an institution

trained for and useful only for defense. Its centralized and depersonalized nature helps

eliminate individualism and ensure cohesion, all of which are necessary for the optimum

performance of its assigned function. However, its authoritarian and undemocratic nature

makes it unfit forstate governance.

Ewlution of Nigerta as A Political Unit Epelle Alafuro 1 9 5

In Nigeria the military has intervened in two epochs in our national history, the first

one being between January 1966 and October 1979 and the second being between December

1983 and May 1999. In each of these instances they have cited as reasons for their

intervention the following

i. Ethnicity and tribal politics of the civilian ruling elites

ii. Corruption of the politicians

iii. Institutional weakness of the socio-political structure of the state.

iv. Under funding of the military institution by the civilians and

v. Invitation by being dissatisfied members of the political class.

Nevertheless, it is obvious that through an objective analysis of the nature and role

of the military when in powe r that the intervention in politics is essential not because

of the above reasons but more rightly because of the following underlisted reasons:

i. Inordinate ambition of the Nigerian military officers

ii. The high premium placed on political power inThird Worl d Countrie s wher e

Politics is seen as a leeway towards primitive accumulation.

iii. Imitative syndrome of Nigerian military officers who will always want to imitate their colleagues in other African countries once such officers assume powers in their respective countries.

The above explains why when the military is in power in Nigeria there tends to be more coups and counter coups by military officers against their colleagues than against civilian regimes. Fortunately, the last military regime headed by Gen. Abdulsalam Abubakar seemed to be an exception to this rule as his regime lasted for only eleven (11) months (June 1998- May 1999) in which he successfully executed a transition programme that led to the emergence of the extant fourth republic.

Presidential Democracy in Nigeria

As stated in the preceding paragraph, the last military rule in Nigeria gave birth to the fourth republic that started on May 29, 1999 with the installation of Chief Olusegun Obasanjo as the Executive President of the country. Sequel to this period, the country had attempted an ill-fated second republic based also on presidential system of government and headed by Alhaji Shehu Shagari of the National Party of Nigeria (NPN). It will be recalled that in that second republic five political parties had contested for various political positions within theNigerian state with the aforementioned NPN winning a majority of the positions at both the state and federal level. The other four parties that had contested at that period were:

Nigerian Peoples Party (NPP)

Great Nigeria Peoples Party (GNPP)

Peoples Redemption Party (PRP)

Unity Party of Nigeria (UPN)

However, with the demis e of that republic on December 31, 1983 the country

Slipped back into military rule with a brief period of an attempted third republic (1991 -1993)

In which two political parties were legislated into existence by the military fiat of the Gen.

Ibrahim Badamosi Babangida regime. The two political parties were the National

Republican convention (NRC) and the Social Democratic Party (SDP). This attempt at a

Evolution of Nigeria as A Political Unit Epelle Alafuro 196

third republic was short lived as the criminal annulment of the June 12 1993 Presidential

Election ostensibly won by Chief Moshood Abiola sparked off a series of social protests

Culminating in the takeover of government by Gen. Sani Abacha. The death of the latter on

June 8, 1998 gave room for the ascendancy to power of the Gen. Abdulsalam Abubakar

Regime who midwives the present fourth republic (Erhagbe 2002:66-70). At the onset of this

Republic many political associations contested for elective positions in the local government

Elections of December 1998 that served as a build up to the eventual general election in

February/March 1999. At the end based on their relative performance e and extent of spread in

The polity the following three political parties were subsequently registered by the

Independent National Electoral Commission (INEC):

i. Alliance for Democracy (AD)

ii. All Peoples Party (APP)

iii. Peoples Democratic Party (PDP)

It is interesting to note that today through a process of alignment, coalition, and realignment the number of political parties in the country has increased to fifty. It is hoped that

As democracy matures, consolidates and becomes more sustainable in the country the

Evolution of the party system in Nigeria will become more stabilized.

CHAPTER SEVEN

CONCLUSION

Concluding Remarks

In conclusion, it is obvious from the analysis above that Nigeria's trajectory towards

a politico-social developed entity had been a long drawn one. Beginning from the pre-colonial era in which state formation was between distinct ethnic entities till the present era,

the country has had rulers who sometimes were exogenous or endogenous. The contribution

of all of these persons brought the country to the stage where we are today. It is believed that

If we are able to shade off centrifugal forces threatening the unity and progress of the country,

Much can still be attained in our drive towards institution building and socio-economic

Progress. The colonialists has done their part, it is now left for us to sec to what extent we can

Build a Nigerian state which we all will be proud of.

Execution of Nigeria as A Political Unit Epelle Alafuro 197

References

Abubakar, S. (1980). Peoples of the Upper Benue Basin and the Bauchi Plateau before

1800 , in Ikime, O, (ed.) Groundwork of Nigerian History, Ibadan: Heinmann.

Ajayi, S.O. (2002). Nigeria History in Pre-colonial Times- Northern Nigeria", in Nzemeke,

AD. and Erhagbe, E.O. (Eds.) Nigerian Peoples and Culture, Benin City: Dept of

History, University of Benin.

Ake, C. (1981). A Political Economy of Africa, London: Longmans.

Ake, C. (1989). The Implications of Military Rule in Nigeria", in Thepolioscope, 5.

Coleman, J.S. (1986). Nigeria: Background to Nationalism, Benin City and Katrineholm:

Broburg and Wistrom.

Crowder, M. (1968). West Africa under Colonial Rule, London, Hutchinson and Co.

Publishers Limited.

Epelle, A. (2010). ^ Colonialism and the Underdevelopment of Nigeria: A Political Economy

Approach", in Icheke: Journal ofthe Faculty of Humanities, 8(1 &2), 11 -20.

Erhagbe, E.O. (2002). "The Dynamics of Evolution of Nigeria as a Political Unit", in

Nzemeke, A. D. and Erhaghe, E.O (eds.) Nigerian Peoples and Culture, Benin City:

Dept of History, University of Benin.

Igwe, U. (2010). "Pre-colonial Political Administrations in Nigeria" in Osuntokun, A.;

Aworawo, D.; Akpan, N.; and Masajuwa, F. (eds.) Issues in Nigerian Government

and Politics, Ibadan: Rex Charles Publications.

Lenin, V. I. (1983). Imperialism: The Highest Stage of Capitalism, Moscow: Progress

Publishers.

Nwabueze, B. O. (1982). A Constitutional History of Nigeria, -London: Longmans.

Osagie, J. I. (2002). "Nigerian History in Pre-colonial Times - Southern Nigeria", in

Nzemeke, A. D. and Erhaghe, E.O. (eds.) Nigerian Peoples and Culture, Benin City:

Dept of History, University of Benin.

Osagie, J. I. and Ikponmwosa, F. (2012). "Nigeria's Pre-colonial Political System", in

Imobighe, T. A., and Ebohon, S. I. (eds.) Themes and Issues in Nigerian

Governance and Politics, Kuru, Jos: National Institute for Policy and Strategic

Studies.

Perham, M. (1957). Native Administration in Nigeria, London: Longman.

www.ingramcontent.com/pod-product-compliance
Lightning Source LLC
Chambersburg PA
CBHW070447220526
45466CB00004B/1779